C000272457

Down to Earth

Mediumship for Sceptics

Teresa Parrott studied Medicine at Southampton University, specialising in Psychiatry as a post-graduate. This included training in individual psychodynamic psychotherapy. She became a Member of the Royal College of Psychiatrists in 1992.

She took a sabbatical from work and moved to Spain. There she met Sue Brotherton. This is the first book they have written together. The sequel is already underway.

Teresa's interests include poetry, playing the piano, and working out.

Sue Brotherton has been acknowledged as one of the top mediums in the UK. When writer and journalist Hazel Courteney received communication from Princess Diana after her death, she asked Sue Brotherton for verification.

Sue has travelled and tutored extensively, demonstrating and leading workshops worldwide. She has also trained as a counsellor and studied transpersonal psychology, which culminated in her developing a unique technique for helping clients.

The mother of two grown-up children, Sue and her husband Dave now live in Spain. Her interests include painting, cooking, and interior design.

Down to Earth

Mediumship for Sceptics

Dr Teresa Parrott
BM, MRCPsych

and

Sue Brotherton
International Medium

Down To Earth
Mediumship For Sceptics
A McDermott Publication

First published in Great Britain in 2005 by
McDermott Publishing Ltd
2 The Green, Kings Norton
Birmingham, B38 8SD
www.mcdermottpublishing.co.uk

Copyright © Teresa Parrott and Sue Brotherton 2005

All rights reserved.
No part of this publication may be reproduced, stored in a retrieval system, or
transmitted, in any form or by any means (including photocopying) without the
prior permission in writing of the authors or the publisher, nor be otherwise
circulated in any form of binding or cover other than that in which it is published
and without a similar condition including this condition being imposed on the
subsequent purchaser. Every effort has been made to ensure the accuracy of the
material within this publication. However, the publisher will not accept any
responsibility for accuracy of content or the opinions expressed by the authors.
This book reflects the personal experience and opinions of the authors and is
intended for interested readers for educational purposes only. In the event that you
use any of the information in this book for yourself, which is your constitutional
right, the authors and the publisher accept no responsibility for your actions.

ISBN 0-9544711-1-3

Cover design and layout
Copyright © McDermott Publishing

Publisher Acknowledgments:
The publisher would like to thank Sue Brotherton and Teresa Parrott
for the inception of *Down to Earth*.
Roger Marshall of Print Publishing Products Limited for his project management,
Julian Day, Linda Perkins of LSP Consultancy, Grant Shipcott of XL Publishing
Services, Christina Lilley of Trapeze Mailing Ltd and Trevor Miles.
Mark Richards of Richards Design for his inspirational cover design.

Photos: Michael Shaw

Printed in Great Britain by Antony Rowe

Dedications

Teresa Parrott
To my mother and my father.

Sue Brotherton
To Dave, my rock.

'Before you start this book, give it the blessing of the spirit world, so that when people read it, they can actually feel the love, the compassion, and the power of spirit touching their hearts. In this book, as in everything, there must be the energy from the spirit world that is all around us, not just the words from the human mind.'

San Lo, Spirit Guide

Contents

Foreword

by Teresa Parrott

I studied Medicine at Southampton University. As a post-graduate, I trained in Psychiatry, including a course in individual psychodynamic psychotherapy, and worked as a psychiatrist for five years, becoming a Member of the Royal College of Psychiatrists in 1992.

Sue Brotherton and I first met in the South of Spain, when I attended one of her workshops on Mediumship and Psychic Awareness. It was February 1998; a pivotal moment in my life.

Five years previously, when I gave up my career in psychiatry, I had moved to Spain. Since then, in a vague kind of way, I had been searching for something. I had just started writing, which had been a secret dream since childhood, but it was all new to me, and there was a lot to learn. In a sense I was waiting to find my next step.

When I went to the workshop, I had no idea what to expect. I'd never spoken to Sue, and I'd never seen a medium working before. In fact I was way out of my comfort zone. Right at the start, I volunteered to go up in front of the group, and she started saying what she sensed from my energy field and unconscious mind. In other words, she started telling me what I thought about myself.

She had never met me before. Within moments, though, she sensed a feeling of fear, loneliness and inadequacy. She told me that I felt constricted, that my tendency to be passive rather than saying what I felt lead to disproportionate tantrums. She said that I was shy and felt quite vulnerable; I found it hard to open up to people till I trusted them, and I had difficulty expressing my emotions. There were parts of myself that I recognised were holding me back, which I needed to let go, in order to free myself.

Sue said that there was a sensitive, compassionate part of me that knew where I was heading, that had strength, power and a capacity for healing and teaching. She also told me (still at this first meeting) that I needed to keep working on myself in order to free the feminine, creative, intuitive side of me, so that it could aid the rational, logical, thinking part. Only then would I accept that, within me, I already had everything that I needed. She told me that I would, finally, get where I wanted to be, and that when I did, it would surpass my wildest dreams.

I was amazed. Within minutes of meeting me, this woman had sensed what it had taken me, a professional psychiatrist, years of self-discovery to learn.

Over the next two days, seeing Sue talk to different people, listening to her views about life and death, and seeing the joy that she felt (and brought to others) when working with spirit, I was convinced that she was a truly kind, sensitive and down to earth person – and an extraordinary medium.

I didn't see her again till five years later, when we decided to write this book.

Sue has been acknowledged for years as one of the top mediums in the UK. She has been working with mediumship for over thirty years, and has given demonstrations and workshops on mediumship, dreams and spiritual/self-growth in many different countries. She has tutored at the Arthur Findlay College for Psychic Studies, and was Chairman of Spiritualist Aid, the charity fund-raising arm of the Spiritualists' National Union. She is a dream-worker and trained counsellor, and has studied transpersonal psychology. She has explored personal and archetypal symbol in great depth, culminating in the development of a unique technique for helping clients to integrate lost aspects of their psyche.

Which is exactly what she helped me to do. After that initial meeting, I joined a writing class and dream group, and spent more and more time writing. I began Reiki and meditation, became a Reiki, Karuna and Seichim Master, and started learning a system of healing called SKHM, which facilitates a direct connection to the energy of Source. I began to feel stronger, more confident, and more able to follow my own intuition.

So I know from personal experience that psychic work and mediumship can change someone's life in most surprising and far-reaching ways.

Yet I still didn't understand it. For years I had been sceptical about mediumship, simply because it was outside the range of my own experience. In terms of mediumship itself, I knew almost nothing – about how being a medium affects a person's life, how it works, what techniques it actually uses. I had many unanswered questions. As many people do.

That's why we chose the question and answer format for this book. Sue talked and I typed. The book is written in her voice; I simply organised the material into what to me seemed a logical order, to guide the reader (and me) step by step on a journey through a lifetime's experience of being a medium.

The book combines, if you like, the logical, organised left brain of a psychiatrist with the creative, volatile right brain of a medium. Although Sue and I have had very different life experiences, and consequently express and interpret those experiences in vastly different ways, it was reassuring to find how much each of our viewpoints made sense to the other. We discovered a great deal of common ground. And, for me, it was a wonderful opportunity to learn.

I learned, for instance, that this broad concept of what we call spirituality can be approached from innumerably different angles. It most certainly does not depend on a particular culture or religion or set of beliefs. Spirituality is a way of being in the world; an appreciation of the many different levels of our mind, body and spirit; an attempt to find meaning in our personal existence and our place in the greater scheme of things.

Spirit is the spark of life that we all have within, that makes us alive and makes us what we each uniquely and individually are. It is the part of us that endures, that lives on after we leave this physical body.

Spirituality is our awareness of, and our attempt to connect to, this divine essence. It is not synonymous with spiritualism.

Spiritualism is a religion which has a set of guiding principles: namely, that the universe is created by the God-force; that at the final stage of evolution of the spirit, or soul, *we are all equal*; that we can communicate with spirit and we all have helpers in the spirit world; that the soul survives physical death and is eternal; that we are responsible for our thoughts and actions and will be our own judges; that recompense must be made for every destructive action, word and thought; and that we always have the opportunity to progress to higher planes of consciousness.

Mediumship is simply the ability to communicate with those in the spirit world. A medium may believe in the spiritualist principles, but does not necessarily subscribe to the spiritualist religion. There are people who have mediumistic abilities but who have no particular interest in the spiritual.

Likewise, a spiritualist is not necessarily a medium. Many people who believe in the spiritualist principles are not mediumistic.

Working with Sue, I also learned what it was like to see a medium communicating directly with a spirit helper. When Sue channelled San Lo, her helper in the spirit world, it was an incredibly moving experience for me. I asked San Lo questions, and she talked to me! I sat typing as fast as I could with tears streaming down my face. She told me many things that I needed to hear.

San Lo claims that she is not highly evolved. But, as Sue later told me, within minutes, she has always been able to reach to the core of people, to their innermost needs and issues. San Lo has infinite compassion and love for people, and it gives her great joy to be with children.

Sue first became aware of San Lo twenty-six years ago. San Lo has always been there when she needed help and guidance, and Sue's understanding and view of both humanity and the spirit world has been very much influenced by San Lo's mind – and the other intelligences from the spirit world that she has helped her to connect with.

San Lo says that she herself is not important, but Sue is convinced that her mediumship would never have developed as it has without her help. For Sue, she has been a mainstay, lifting her through some very dark patches, showing her constant and unconditional love, and a joy that is beyond this earth.

As I write this passage, San Lo is telling Sue and me that it is the message of compassion and love that is all-important. Everybody has the capacity to love, and to be compassionate to others, once they are free to be themselves. That compassion and love will show itself in many guises, as each individual comes to express it in his or her own unique and individual way.

Many people are fascinated by mediumship and psychic phenomena. They know that more exists than just the material side of life, and they may themselves have experienced happenings that they cannot explain. This book, drawing upon one medium's experiences over thirty years of working with mediumship, will reassure them that they are not alone!

Many people today are actively seeking a spiritual pathway. One that is not limited by rules and dogma, but which fits their own intuitive knowledge. This book is intended for all those who are interested in finding out more about what will happen to them after death, and who are searching for ways of discovering more about who they truly are in life. Whether mediums or spiritualists – or sceptics.

We all come from different starting points. We interpret ourselves and our lives in the light of our unique experiences, backgrounds, and beliefs. So we will all have different questions.

This book aims to answer… well at least some of them.

Life after Death

Introduction

Death is not the end of everything. We don't just shuffle off and disappear. When our physical body dies, we are still alive. We have consciousness, we have experiences, and we can affect others, just not in quite the same way as when we're here on earth.

The spirit is the energy that makes up a person; the thoughts and feelings, the memories and experiences, the joys and sorrows that make each of us what we uniquely are. When we pass to the other world, the physical body is left behind, but the life force, the spirit or spark of life that we all have, continues to exist, and to be meaningful.

Most of us here on earth cannot sense a person in spirit. That's because when we leave this world to pass into the spirit world, our energy, or vibrational rate, changes to a frequency that is outside of the normal range of the five senses.

Science has shown that everything, including matter, is energy. The physical body is merely energy vibrating at a rate that falls within the range of our physical senses.

Scientific evidence demonstrates that energy is flowing through us all the time. Our body is surrounded by an electromagnetic field, or aura, which is energy vibrating at a higher level than that of our physical body.

The spirit world is in fact constantly sending energy and thoughts and love out to us. It's just that most of us are not able to tune in to receive those messages.

A medium is someone who can increase his or her own vibrational rate so that he or she can sense the higher vibrational rate of those in spirit. By entering into an altered state of consciousness, or trance, s/he becomes open to direct communication from spirit.

Not only can mediums sense a person in the spirit world, they can also tune in to his or her energy to find out exactly who that person is.

A medium therefore acts as a bridge between human beings and the world of spirit. As I see it, the job of a medium is to be of service to those in spirit; to bring comfort to people here by letting them know that they still exist, and to help them to give messages to their loved ones.

A medium gives people convincing personal proof of the existence of life after death. This can radically change the way that they approach their life.

Spirit on Earth

We live in a world that places great value on the physical, material things that we can see and touch and explain, rather than the invisible, mysterious things of the spirit that we have more difficulty in sensing and understanding, yet that we are nonetheless able to experience.

When our physical body dies, our consciousness lives on. Yet many people find this hard to believe.

Most of us think we're pretty rational, sensible, down to earth people. Our logical minds think they know all there is to know. But they don't. There are many experiences that we can't explain. Our logical minds don't have all the answers.

This is actually very good news, because whatever our minds keep telling us – that this is all there is, or that there's no great purpose beyond ourselves – inside, in our quiet moments when our minds are still, when we allow ourselves to truly feel, we know that secretly we wish there was more. Being honest, we know we're missing something.

We only have to find it. There is a part of us, separate from our physical body, which is meaningful and alive. This is our spiritual essence, if you like. We can't necessarily sense it through our physical senses. We can't necessarily explain or understand it using the reason and logic of our rational minds. Yet it is there.

The wonderful thing is that while we're living in our physical bodies, now, here on earth, we're also, all of us, already spiritual beings. We all have a spirit within.

It's just that we treat it a bit like a poor relation. We don't take much notice of it, we're not that interested in what it has to say, we don't like our friends to see it.

We quite like our bodies; they make us feel good, we can wear nice clothes, people comment on how we look. Our minds are okay too, they learn and remember, they win arguments, and we can use them in all sorts of clever ways to impress people.

But our spirit is the life force that makes us alive. It's the powerful energy that gives us passion and enthusiasm and the will to achieve our purpose and make our dreams reality. It is the gentle, soothing energy that allows us to forgive our mistakes and weaknesses, to view others with compassion, and to heal our pain. And it's the beautiful, joyful energy that enables us to love, and to know that we are not alone.

All of us have, at some time in our lives, felt moments of despair, when, forgetting that we are spirit, we are overwhelmed with a sense of loneliness and longing.

When we lose our sense of our own spirit, we feel as if we have lost our very centre. Everything becomes a struggle; we experience pain and yet we don't know what to do about it; we feel isolated, as if no one in the world can reach into what we're experiencing, and we can't reach out of ourselves to find any source of comfort or help.

Our spirit is our consciousness; it drives us to question, to learn, to find meaning in our experiences. It is the place where everything comes together, where everything makes sense, where we are not separate and alone but together, connected and purposefully intertwined. Becoming aware of our own spirit, we feel that we are loved, that our lives have purpose, that we are part of a forgiving world.

Often it is fear that stops us from recognising our own spirituality. We don't ask questions because we fear the answers. We don't give ourselves enough quiet time in which to come to understand who we really are and what we are capable of. In fact, the problem is that we don't really trust ourselves. Fear constantly limits our possibilities. Then, worst of all, because we're afraid of the spiritual dimensions within ourselves, we say they don't exist. We deny the fact that there is spiritual life within life itself.

So, just for a moment, we need to suspend fear. We can trust ourselves, for we already have all the answers within us. At some level, we already know much more than we give ourselves credit for.

The first message of this book is simply that we are all spiritual beings. Our spirit is the life force that exists at the centre of our very being. It is the God force, which brings us love and healing, joy and compassion; the divine spark that creates our whole being and connects us to every other living thing in this immense and beautiful universe.

The second message is that we need have no fear of death. The truth is that when we leave our physical body, we are still alive.

Our beliefs often preclude us from hearing these messages. Many people are sceptical, simply saying, 'I don't believe in an afterlife.' But then, just fifty years ago most people believed it was impossible to send a man to the moon. As has occurred in so many endeavours throughout history, a few people challenged the old beliefs and pursued their vision – with spectacular results.

Today, at a global level, communication systems, technology and science are advancing so rapidly that old beliefs are being redefined all the time. At an individual level, we're constantly reviewing and renewing our beliefs in the light of new knowledge and experience.

So we need not worry too much about beliefs just at this point, because we never know when they're going to change. What we do know is that we can choose what we believe. It's as simple as that. Believing that something is possible, it becomes possible, and as our beliefs change, so too does our reality.

It's true also that our belief system can change instantly without any thought at all. Something happens – like watching a startling sunset, or listening to beautiful music, seeing a newborn baby, drifting out of body in meditation, or falling in love for the first time. Our whole world suddenly seems to expand.

Such reality shifts are awesome, and tend to be unnerving. We're likely to find ourselves, as Douglas Adams so beautifully says, 'as stunned as a man might be who, having believed himself to be totally blind for five years, suddenly discovers that he had merely been wearing too large a hat.'*

Just for a moment, we glimpse the vastness of the universe, the beauty of creation, the joy of our own spirit. We feel as if we've been touched by the gods. And we probably have.

Oftentimes, of course, things go at a slower rate. With the legacy of fear and doubt and distrust that many of us carry, we plod along for years feeling as if we're not really getting anywhere. We can want things to change, yet we can't seem to make anything happen. Or we simply don't feel ready.

That's when we could do with a bit of help. So why not ask?

The spirit world around us is always at our service. There are those in spirit who dearly want to help mankind. It's just that they operate at a higher vibration than we do, so we are not always convinced that we're receiving the energy and thoughts that they send to us. Often, with the denser, heavier energy associated with our physical body, we're not at the right frequency to receive them. We are so stressed out by the distractions of the external world, or so tied up in the repetitive worries of our conscious minds, that we can't hear anything else.

---

* Douglas Adams, *So Long, And Thanks For All The Fish*, Pan Books Ltd, 1984.

But it is possible for us, here on earth, to free our consciousness and become more closely attuned to our spiritual essence. Then we're far more likely to be able to tune in to the energy frequency of those in the spirit world.

There are many different ways of raising our own vibration to achieve this. By meditating, we switch off to the distractions of the outside world and the distracting thoughts of our own minds, and become aware of ourselves simply as energy. By praying from the heart, or by connecting to healing energy, we can raise our vibration. Sometimes it happens spontaneously when we go into a trance-like state, daydreaming, when our conscious minds are tied up in mundane things and our unconscious minds are open and receptive to energies outside of us.

The energy of those who have passed into the other world, the world where the physical body no longer exists, is lighter, finer, of a higher frequency, so it's easier for these spirit beings to channel healing energies and connect to other minds within the spirit world. And, when our minds are in a meditative, dreamy, trance-like state, it's easier for them to connect to us. Mind to mind, or spirit to spirit, connection is always possible, it's just that most of the time most of us here on earth are not in that state long enough or often enough for that communication to get through.

But we have all experienced it. Even just in fleeting moments, there are times when we have a sense of something touching us in some way. We feel, not through our senses but with our sixth sense, that there is something there. We experience a hunch, a gut feeling, that we cannot explain. Or a moment of inspiration, when a thought or image comes to our minds that we know did not originate within ourselves. Without thinking, an insight just pops into our mind and we suddenly understand something with greater clarity than ever before.

That's why we are more creative when our unconscious minds are open and receptive to energies, ideas and images outside our normal range of conscious awareness.

Anyone who has worked creatively will be aware of these moments of sudden inspiration or understanding, moments when, through our intuition, we receive knowledge or insight from outside of ourselves. Many poets, artists, musicians and philosophers have described this throughout history. It is as if a greater force is acting through them. They're not doing it on their own.

It seems that a hierarchy, an evolutionary or guidal chain, exists through which higher energies, greater wisdom, and a deeper understanding of love pass downward. The point is, we all have the capability to experience the spirit world in one or other of its facets.

We just have to be in the right frame of mind. We have to do the groundwork, the preparation, which really means the work on ourselves. As with any creative act we must learn the basic techniques, whether of art or music, writing or meditation. We prepare the ground by learning and practising till we master the craft. We clear our minds of distracting thoughts and worries, and trust in our unconscious or intuitive mind, which can then reach into itself to discover something new and beautiful, and also reach out from itself to connect with the knowledge that exists in the universe around us, the energies and ideas and wisdom of all those who have gone before us. In this way we are part of this guidal chain, part of this spiritual consciousness.

And this too is what happens when a medium is contacting the spirit world. By entering into an altered state of consciousness, or trance, and, if an audience is present, by also using some of the group energy to raise his or her rate of vibration, s/he becomes open to direct communication from spirit.

What happens when we die

A lot of people are afraid to think about life after death. Certainly they never talk about death; it's a taboo subject in the Western world. There are two separate issues to consider here.

Firstly there are the circumstances that lead to the actual death of the physical body. This is the winding down of the physical body, as it becomes old or diseased or unable to function any more. Many of us fear that we might experience illness and pain before we die. We all hope that when we go it will be a quick and painless process; none of us wants to suffer or lose our dignity. Ideally, we'd all like to slip away peacefully in our sleep. Sadly, that's not always the case.

Secondly, there is what happens at the exact moment of death of the physical body. This is the moment of transition from life on earth, where we exist in both physical and spiritual form, to life afterwards, where we exist in purely spirit form. This passage into the next world can be a joyous experience, or it can come as a bit of a shock. It all depends on the individual.

I always use the analogy of going on holiday. If I were planning a trip to South America, I would talk to people who'd been there, I'd read books and find out what it's like. The climate, sights to see, places to eat. I would be excited, but I would also want to be prepared for what I might find. Many people would do that too. But when it comes to looking into what will happen to them on their journey through life and beyond, most people are too scared to do it.

I know that I'm going to go on the greatest journey of my life, that this is just the beginning of a fantastic voyage. For people who accept and know that there is life after death, death holds no fear. They need only to simply let go, for, on the other side of life, there will be someone to greet them, someone who loves them, whom they will recognise and run to and put their arms around. It will be a joyful experience.

But for some people, it's a shock, particularly those who've never believed in the afterlife, or those who've died suddenly, for example in an accident, as a result of suicide or murder, or from sudden and unexpected illness. They've had no time to get used to the idea.

In these instances, what often happens is that they'll see a friend from long ago, or a pet, and they may not see family for a little while until they have recovered from the shock of no longer being alive in a physical body. But there will still be people on the other side who will look after them. In some cases, if they're in hospital when they pass over, they find themselves in a hospital bed with doctors and nurses going about their work. Their minds recreate their surroundings, so that something is familiar, then a pet might appear, or a relative will come, and they are slowly helped to accept the fact that they are on the other side of life.

I did a sitting in London once, in which I knew I'd got a contact with an old lady in spirit, but I couldn't make out what she was saying; her words were really jumbled and her sentences were jumping all over the place. I described her to the woman who had come for the sitting, and she said that it was her mother, who had had Alzheimer's before she died. The old lady had not yet come to the realisation that she no longer needed to be constrained by the limitations of the illness now that she no longer had a physical body.

There's no golden rule about how long that takes; some people take longer than others to come to an awareness that they are now able to be whole again.

When people have suffered from mental or physical illness, or brain disease, before they pass over, it takes time for them to adjust to the fact that in the spirit world we can create anything we want through the power of our minds. We can go back to a disease-free state; we can become again who we truly were inside, despite the ravages of the illness process. But it doesn't happen overnight.

People coming for a sitting are often upset because their loved one who was dying was unable to respond to what they said or did in their last moments together. If the person was unconscious by the time they got to the hospital or even found out that they were ill, they would often feel bad that they did not have the chance to speak and say goodbye. But in the sitting, the person in spirit will frequently say, 'I heard you, I knew you were there,' even though s/he was unable to show any recognition or response at the time.

For all of us, at the moment that we pass over, there are those in the spirit world who are guiding what's going to happen next. They will bring in the animals and people you knew to get you gradually accustomed to the fact that you still exist but not in the physical sense. After all, your body has been the focus of your persona for a long time. You've got used to it. So it can take some time to get used to being without it now that you exist simply as energy.

When you pass into the spirit world, you're going to leave your body behind, and you're going to miss it, you know. It's like stepping out of a suit of clothes you've worn for a very long time. Or taking a jelly out of a mould and finding it still stands on its own. You thought that your body was all you had, yet it was in fact just the container. Your body contained your energy, your life force, and when that container is gone, the energy is still there, it's just no longer contained. It's free to take up any shape it likes. Or to remain shapeless. To move, or to stay still. It can do whatever you want it to.

What people in the spirit world do

I have often been asked, what do people do in the spirit world? Basically, the answer is that they have free choice.

At first, the vast majority carry on living the sort of life that they lived on earth. Their minds recreate their homes, their pets, their familiar surroundings, and they just get on with their own thing. They go about their daily lives, they bump into people they know are dead, and eventually they will accept that they are in the spirit world. Each being takes his or her own time to accept and adjust to passing into spirit.

I remember one woman who told me that whenever she had a bath, she would place three flannels over her private parts because she was afraid that spirits might be watching her. I tend to think that the spirit world's perception of us has to be on a different level to that; maybe they just know what we've been doing, without having to be actually present. Quite frankly, if anyone came to see me having a bath they'd go away laughing their socks off.

We're judging the spirit world by our own standards all the time, imagining that they might want to do this or that, and of course, maybe some will.

When we pass to the spirit world, we're still concerned about those left behind. I don't think that hinders our journey. But we do also want to expand our consciousness. That doesn't mean that those in spirit can't keep in touch with us here, just as if you lived on the other side of the world you could still be in touch with your family. But those of us on earth are just one part of an awareness that's now expanding.

People on earth will often be drawn to different groups or people of like mind. This is the same when we pass.

On the other hand, there are relationships here which, however long we have tried to make them work, just do not improve. Some people simply are never going to get on with each other. This applies in the spirit world too. We don't all love our 'loved ones;' for some of us the thought of spending eternity with certain members of our family is not appealing at all. We could spend the rest of our time on earth trying to overcome these differences, becoming more and more frustrated. Or we can accept that it's just best to let those relationships or friendships go.

Just because it is possible to communicate with others in the spirit world directly through thought or intent, does not mean that we have to. In the spirit world, we can choose with whom to communicate. We can choose what we think about. We can meet people of like mind, and we can spend our time exercising free choice in a way that is not being overlooked or invaded by other people. The point is, as we take greater responsibility for ourselves, we come to look at a wider range of options than we could conceive were possible on earth. We become aware of possibilities that we couldn't even contemplate before. In the spirit world, we can choose where our consciousness goes.

There are many in the spirit world who still want to assist people on earth with their skills. Gordon Higginson, for instance, was one of the finest mediums in the UK and President of the Spiritualists' National Union. Gordon has spent many years trying to help mediums to reach their full potential, both in life and from the spirit world.

If there were things that we believed in and enjoyed doing during our life on earth, ways in which we were creative or caring or know-ledgeable, then in the spirit world we're still able to do them. There are certainly doctors, writers and artists in the spirit world who are working through the minds of people on earth to help them to expand their capabilities. Many doctors are still helping with healing; surgeons in spirit still use their skills, working with healers within the auric field of people to bring about amazing results.

In fact, whatever our skill, we can still help from the other side. Sally came to see me after her lover died. He was an accountant, and had been a businessman, and he died suddenly of a heart attack, leaving behind unresolved financial matters that she didn't know what to do with.

During our sessions, he spoke to me, and guided her through two years of a very delicate financial and business mess. His name was Bob, and he told me that if I needed any more help on financial matters, just to call on him.

He'd been a very smart and romantic man; they used to go on cruises and dance together, and he liked Mantovani. One day Sally phoned me in great excitement, and said she'd just played the tape I'd made of our previous session. On it, she had distinctly heard Mantovani playing in the background.

Bob was a kind man who would help anybody. Often after that, if I was seeing people with financial worries, I would ask for his help. He would appear, still happy to share his business knowledge from the other side. I would be able to slip into his mind and get some financial advice.

Many people in spirit will spend time doing things they always wanted to do or going to places they always wanted to visit. For those who were physically restricted or in pain, there is the delight of being pain-free, of being able to move again, and they just enjoy dancing and swimming, playing sport, being young again, and they may stay doing these things for a long time. This is difficult for us to understand because although we measure time, in the spirit world there is no time. A year could feel like a minute.

But, however time is experienced, there will gradually come a moment when those spirit beings will start to think there is more than this and their consciousness will start to shift.

Every person here on earth builds their own world through their own state of mind. In the spirit world, too, we create our own world, we can build a world that we always wanted, or we can recreate our home; the possibilities are limitless. When we pass to the spirit world we still have free will. We are still locked into whatever limitations we impose upon ourselves. Heaven and hell are indeed a state of mind. We continue to be able to change and have realisations when we've gone to the spirit world. So when a person passes to spirit they may grow and become more aware of themselves and become able to say and do and think things they weren't able to during their life on earth.

There is no sudden transformation of our personality or emotions or beliefs just because we've passed into the spirit world. We continue to learn at the rate that is appropriate for us, in ways that we determine for ourselves. Once we free ourselves of some of our anger and pain, our guilt and blame, we can then start our beautiful journey into the next stage of awareness, when our consciousness shifts to a higher level.

What it means when we sense a spirit

Many people, when they have lost loved ones, still sense them. When they're doing mundane things like washing up or mowing the lawn, when their conscious mind isn't in control, they slip into a trance-like state. In this altered state of consciousness, they are able to sense the spirit world and they may catch a glimpse or feel the presence of their loved one in spirit. However, many people believe that such an experience means that something bad is going to happen.

Not so long ago one elderly lady I know was really upset at the breakdown of her grand-daughter's marriage. She claimed that it was all her fault. I wondered how this could be, as they lived many miles apart and had little contact. When I asked her, she said that she had seen her long-dead mother in a dream and had spoken to her. To her mind, the break-up of the marriage was the retribution she had to pay for talking to her mother in the dream. I said if that were the case, my whole life would have been filled with great traumas! I reassured her that it's perfectly natural to talk in dreams to people in spirit. When we're dreaming, the barriers to communication with the spirit world are lowered.

There's nothing to fear when we sense something from the spirit world. They're not bearers of bad news. Many people still see them as bad luck, as figments of their imagination or, particularly if they don't believe in the afterlife, they simply just ignore them. This can be very confusing and upsetting for the person in the spirit world. There they are in their home, with their family and friends, yet no one speaks to them. People on earth sometimes act as if those in spirit are sitting around on a cloud playing a harp. Well, maybe they find the harp difficult to master and actually merely want to carry on being around the ones they love.

From the many people in spirit that I have had the privilege to talk with it seems that there is nothing they like better than still to be involved in their family's life. They very much see themselves as still part of the family, and they want to join in with the good times and put in their two penniesworth when things are going badly.

So many have said how much they enjoy the fact that their family still talk to them, still have a good old moan at them, still ask, 'What on earth shall I do now?'

It's a good idea just to talk to the people in the spirit world; include them in our daily thoughts, chat to them in our minds, moan and carry on as we would if they were standing in front of us. Don't treat them as if they've disappeared. It can be very frustrating for people on the other side of life not to be acknowledged.

Happily, many people send out these thoughts even if they do not voice them out loud, in which case those on the other side of life hear them, and are thankful that they have not been forgotten.

Once we accept that there is life after death, we need not feel so miserable and hopeless about death. We begin to see it in a different light when we know that our loved ones still exist and are still around us.

Those in spirit often say to me, 'Thank you for talking to me.' They like to be talked to and involved in everyday things. We just need to remember that we can still talk to them, even though we may not get an answer straight away!

There used to be a belief, perhaps related to the Christian story of the Resurrection, that people in spirit cannot communicate for three days after death. However, in my experience, they can communicate just as soon as they've died.

A friend of mine had a phone call from the hospital saying that her brother-in-law had died suddenly. He was in his early forties, and had had a heart attack while on the rugby field. As she was too upset to drive, I went to her house to take her to the Queen Elizabeth Hospital in Birmingham.

I only knew her brother-in-law from conducting his marriage service in the Spiritualist Church. While we were driving, I became aware of him. I heard the name Newey & Eyre, a company I knew simply as an electrical wholesaler. I told her the name, and at the same time I remember saying, 'He must have been a really cheeky chap, he's playing with the clips on your bra.'

'I can't believe it,' she said, 'he's only just died and he's already talking to us! He's worked at Newey & Eyre for years, and they made clips for bras.' He was speaking to me all the time as we made our way to the hospital. And later, the following day, when I visited his wife, who was devoted to him, he spoke to her too, and this brought her great comfort.

I've also seen someone looking very well and in his best clothes, standing by his coffin as he was being cremated.

So there is no set time you have to wait until a spirit can communicate. Both of these people had an open mind and an acceptance of life after death. They were therefore able to communicate straight away.

I remember when we first moved into our house. I woke up and there was an old lady standing by the side of my bed, so I started talking to her in my mind. Dave, my husband, woke too, and asked, 'What's happening?'

I replied, 'There's a lady by the bed and she used to live in the house. She doesn't like the way it's all been altered.'

I explained to her that *we* lived here now, and said, 'Sorry, the house can still be the same for you. But, you know, there is another world that you can go to, where your family and friends are waiting for you.'

There was a farm and a row of four houses, originally built in

Victorian times for the farmer's children, on the site of an old Roman village. Our house was one of the four houses, and one of the neighbours was an elderly man who had lived there for years. I told him what had happened, and described the woman I'd seen, and he said, 'Oh yes, that's the woman who used to live there.' He remembered her clearly.

The old lady had been upset at the changes that were going on in the house. The chat I had with her obviously put her mind at rest, because I was never aware of her again. Often, in an old building, people will see a spirit, sometimes in solid form, and they think that the spirit is appearing for them. But it may just be someone who lived there, or in a house that previously occupied that site, merely going about his own business.

If I hadn't talked to the old lady and found out what was troubling her, I could have imagined all sorts of things about her, her reason for being there, her state of mind. Or she might have kept appearing if she felt no one were taking any notice of her. I didn't mind if she wanted to stay around, but I didn't want her to feel upset about something that was so easily rectified.

The point is that you can't assume anything just from the fact that someone is there. It's easy to say they're stuck, or they should have moved on, but if they are just there because they want to be there and they're not upset about anything, then fine. If they are distressed about something, it's nice if you can find out what it is and see if you can do something to smooth things over.

If someone in the spirit world is having difficulty accepting that they've passed, then the emotional energy of that spirit can start making things happen that people find disturbing. If no one can sense the spirit, or if no one is talking to him or her, that spirit may feel ignored and frustrated. He or she may start to make things move around the house purely out of frustration, or in an attempt to be noticed.

There was one instance in which drawers kept opening and objects kept moving. A medium was asked to investigate. It turned out that a woman had died there in childbirth and she, obviously in great distress, was looking for her baby. The medium was able to help the mother, by explaining what had happened and by trying to find out where the child was.

At other times, I have found that paranormal phenomena are merely due to the memory of strong emotions imprinted on the fabric of a building. This can be the case particularly in very old buildings such as castles and mansions, and it may lead people to believe that they are haunted.

Not all instances of things moving around are due to the spirit world. Sometimes it's the energy of people *here* that causes it to happen.

As soon as I set foot in a house I know if there have been a lot of arguments, or if there are pubertal children with a lot of energy. I can tap into the energy and feel that it is from the human world not the spirit world. Sometimes it builds to such an extent that it can make pictures fall off the wall or doors bang. Strange things happening in the house can often be due to the psychic energy from tension, stress, or conflict.

Similarly, I can feel the energy of the spirit world. I visited a house recently to see the sister of someone who used to come to me for sittings. She and her husband were both teachers, and they were nervous, wondering if the house was haunted. They would find things had been moved in the kitchen; oranges had been taken out of the fruit bowl, or there was a trail of sweet papers from a jar of sweets. Their children had reported that pencils had gone missing from the table at which they were sitting, or their teddy bears had been moved. Once they found a china ornament, which was usually on the window-sill in the bathroom, placed down the loo. Amazingly, it wasn't broken.

I half expected it to be the energy of the people in the house, so I was surprised to see a little girl riding up and down the hall on one of the old red Triang tricycles with solid wheels. She was delightful, cheerfully playing in the house that she had lived in when she was alive. I talked to her, and realised that she had Down's syndrome. She told me she liked sitting by the woman's son while he was playing. They were energetic kids.

We went into the lounge, and I told the woman what I'd seen. Far from being alarmed at the prospect of a 'ghost' in her house, she seemed relieved to know what the phenomenon was. While we were chatting, the little girl came up and leaned on the side of the sofa, holding a white fluffy toy, a rabbit, listening to what was being said about her, and she was quite happy.

I was wondering what to do next. Sitting quietly, asking for help, I became aware of my spirit guide, San Lo. She said, 'Leave it to me.' San Lo loves children. Suddenly the room was filled with spirit children of the same age as the girl. They came into the centre of the room, and started playing 'ring a ring of roses'. The little girl was overjoyed to join in the game, and she went off to play with them. San Lo said as they drifted out together, 'We'll take care of her now, but I can't be sure she won't come back.' I never found out whether she did or not.

Some people, when they sense spirit, don't like to talk to whoever it is because they feel they might be holding them back. By encouraging them to be around, they feel they might be stopping them from moving on. Many people are under the impression that communicating with dead people somehow impedes their progress on the other side or prevents them from achieving peace. In my experience nothing is further from the truth.

In fact, if we sense people around us, it doesn't mean they're always there, they can still be off doing other things. It certainly doesn't mean that they are what some people have come to label 'earthbound.'

When they were alive on earth, we were just a part of their lives, and the same is true when they are in spirit. They still have other things to be dealing with, it's not that they're spending all their time with us.

They may want to communicate with us, because they shared so much with us and we are still a part of their emotional life. They may want to show us that they still love us, or they might want to help us. There may be things they can't yet say to us. They, just like us, are grappling with many changes, not least of which is getting used to existing without a body.

It's not for us to decide who needs to move on and who doesn't. The best thing that we can do when we sense spirits is to talk to them, tell them the things that we want to say, and maybe we'll be encouraged to open ourselves more to the possibilities of our own spirituality. Just as the spirit world tries to reach out to your mind, so you can reach out with your mind, sending your consciousness to another level in order to learn about the spirit world.

CHAPTER TWO

Discovering Mediumship:
The Medium Answers the Psychiatrist

Chapter Outline

What is mediumship?

When did you first discover you were a medium?

How did you feel when you first contacted the spirit world?

How did you practise and develop your mediumship?

Does your mediumship always work when you want it to?

How do you switch your mediumship on and off?

What does it feel like when you're contacting spirit?

Do you have to be in an altered state of consciousness?

What is a spirit?

If I don't believe in the afterlife, what will happen when I die?

How has being a medium affected your life?

What do you believe is the purpose of life?

What is mediumship?

When people are developing their mediumship, they start to become aware of something, which they naturally assume is the spirit world. But it isn't always. All mediums are psychic (although not all psychics are mediums) so it may be that instead they are picking up the thoughts, feelings and energy of people here on earth.

After that initial exhilaration, when they are just discovering for themselves that there is life after death, one of the problems that mediums face is determining whether the vibration they are sensing is coming from the spirit world or coming from people in the physical world. It is not without a lot of hard work that we can tell the difference.

Generally speaking, mediums, although intelligent, operate more from the creative right brain as opposed to the logical, rational left brain. We have to work very hard to integrate our left brain, our logical thinking mind. On the other hand, people who are coming essentially from their left hemisphere would have great difficulty in sensing spirit because, questioning everything they sensed, they would probably dismiss much of it.

The problem is that the left brain constantly interferes with mediumship; a logical person will keep analysing and dissecting what they are experiencing, or their thinking mind will simply tell them that the spirit world doesn't exist.

A medium is usually quite an imaginative and creative person; we don't always make the best business people. A medium's mind has to be free, as opposed to being weighed down with facts and figures and logic. Being more right-brained, we simply have to sense and experience, and not let the need for explanations and reasons interfere when we're working.

So although it is necessary for a medium, at some time, to look logically and critically at what happened within a sitting or demonstration, it's important to do this afterwards, not when it's actually happening, so as not to interfere with the communication.

There's an interesting parallel between mediumship and acting. When actors are learning a role they have to get into character, which means that they put aside their own personality for a time and take on the attributes, character traits and history of someone else. This is exactly what a medium has to do.

When working with spirit, I become a channel for whoever is

communicating. What I am, personally, is put aside. I take on the persona of that person in spirit, and I'm not aware of myself in the normal way. In a demonstration I could have eight or ten different spirits using my abilities to express themselves and their needs.

Many mediums share with actors and other performing artists the volatility of the artistic temperament. When I was working full-time with mediumship, doing workshops, demonstrations and private sittings, I could become quite the prima donna because of the heightened sensitivity and reactivity associated with mediumship.

Since I've stopped working, most things just wash over me, but when something frustrates me, I often think that had I still been working, my prima donna would have instantly emerged.

A lot of energy is required in order to communicate with the spirit world. Many mediums bring up energy through the root chakra to increase their personal energy. The root chakra, at the base of the spine, is the first of the seven major chakras, or energy centres, of the body. The Eastern model of the human energy system is that we each have interconnecting energy centres through which our energy constantly flows. The root chakra grounds us and connects us to the earth: it is a source of powerful energy.

In mediumship, therefore, the root chakra becomes strengthened to the extent that we can get angry very quickly and can also become very sexual beings. This isn't the case with every medium, but is certainly true of some.

There is a belief that a medium is a highly evolved and spiritual being, but I'm afraid that's not the case. Mediumship is a capability that mediums are born with, in the same way that certain singers or artists or musicians are born with the ability to perform, but spirituality and mediumship do not necessarily go together.

The spiritual side of the medium has to be developed in the same way that everyone else's does. The medium's life is fraught with as many ups and downs and problems as anyone else's. Through our own work on ourselves, we all have to find compassion, and it's only when we're at one with ourselves, and with God, that we can find the real joy in life and within people, and become forgiving and compassionate beings.

When did you first discover you were a medium?

I discovered that I had mediumistic abilities when I was about thirty. Up until then, I'd always been afraid of anything to do with mediumship, although I knew that my grandmother was a natural medium.

As I've already said, a natural medium is born, just like a natural artist, but it may be some time before that person becomes aware of their capability. Although a fair number of people have mediumistic abilities, some develop them and others don't. Of those that do develop them, there are still some to whom it comes more easily than others.

When I was teaching mediumship classes, I always used the analogy of learning a musical instrument. Many people take violin lessons. Some will become good enough to play in an orchestra. A few become solo violinist. But how many Nigel Kennedys are there?

As with most things, mediumship requires a combination of natural ability and hard work. One without the other is just not enough. A medium has a responsibility both to people here on earth and to those in the spirit world. Therefore, I feel very strongly that it's unethical and dangerous for people to work with mediumship who are just scratching the surface.

I had to do it to the best of my ability. I had to be as honest as I could. I also had to work hard on myself to be able to trust fully what I was sensing, to know that it was coming from the spirit world and not from my own psyche, or that of other people.

That caused me great stress over the years. If you make a contact with the spirit world for a particular person, and you get it wrong, that person may, in this life, never have another chance to talk to their loved one again. Which can cause a great deal of frustration to those in the spirit world.

It's a big responsibility and if you get it wrong, you can't simply put it right later.

I was very self-critical simply because I wanted to do it well. In mediumship, the perfectionist aspect of me played a big part. In the physical world making mistakes was something I could accept. Although I didn't like letting people down, I could own up and it didn't worry me. But in mediumship it did. I'd be devastated if I thought I had let the spirit world down.

People would say to me, 'I've been to other mediums, but you're the only one my mother will talk through.' And that could have made my head swell! But communication with a particular person is not just dependent on the medium. The spirit's personality will also determine the ability to work through different mediums. So, if the mother's personality is compatible with mine, she'll talk to me.

I don't believe that a medium is capable of contacting everybody in the spirit world, simply because we don't always gel. The spirit may not like the medium, and if there is a personality clash, he won't want to communicate. It's exactly the same as with people here. If I don't like someone, I'm not going to share my own intimate memories and emotions with him, and why would it change in the spirit world?

It's interesting that in the many private sittings I had for myself, no one was ever able to communicate with any of my family in spirit. In fact, there have only ever been two occasions when I have received a message from spirit for myself.

So I can quite understand when people say that life after death doesn't exist. Apart from the first experience when I was thirty – when I went to a demonstration and, unexpectedly, the medium said he had a message from my grandmother – and the last – when my father communicated at a demonstration in Bromsgrove – when I was fifty-nine, no evidence of life after death was given to me personally at all. Throughout my working life as a medium, all the messages I received were for other people's benefit.

As I'm a very private person, it might have been that I was blocking that communication; maybe I wasn't open enough; maybe my tutor part was too strong, or my perfectionist part was insisting that they had to get it right. I wasn't willing to accept hazy descriptions. Vague references to life after death do not, to me, constitute proof.

Graham Lymer, a lovely man from Stoke-on-Trent, was the medium on that second occasion, and I shall be eternally grateful to him. Because he gave me overwhelming proof about my father. He was demonstrating in the Spiritualist Church in Bromsgrove, in Worcestershire; the church is a beautiful small converted chapel, with a very caring and spiritual committee and congregation.

Graham announced from the platform that I had been his tutor at the College of Psychic Studies, and that my dad had a message for me. He talked about my dad's amazing sense of humour, gave a physical description of him down to the Old Spice aftershave that he always wore, and gave many little details that proved without a doubt that it was my dad. He mentioned that my brother had just joined him in the spirit world. He said that my dad understood the very stressful situation that I was experiencing, that he backed me all the way, and that I should move to Spain as I had planned.

It may sound strange, but it wasn't until then that I fully realised what a difference a contact from the spirit world can make. Over the years, people have often said to me, 'You've helped so many people,' but I was never aware of that at a personal level. Working with mediumship, you can't remember afterwards the details of what happened, and you don't know how it feels for someone at the time that they are receiving the contact.

That occasion with Graham Lymer was the first time that I really realised what people were talking about. It was the first time I felt that I had truly helped others. I was going through a difficult time in my life, and it was only when, in my mind, I was desperately begging and pleading with my dad to speak to me, that he did finally communicate with me through the medium. And it meant the world to me.

How did you feel when you first contacted the spirit world?

I've never won the lottery, I rarely even win a raffle, but I can't remember ever being as excited as I was on that day. It was mind-blowing.

Up until then, I had always been afraid of dying. Even when I went to a medium for a private sitting for the first time, I was still absolutely terrified.

When I was thirty, after my dad had died and I had received the message from my grandmother in spirit, I started to go to a mediumship development circle. After I'd been going for a few months, I was lying in bed one night next to Dave, and I suddenly became aware of his grandfather standing by the side of the bed. I woke Dave, and described what I had seen.

The man was wearing prominent green eyeshades, like croupiers used to wear years ago. Dave said, 'Yes, that's my grandad. He used to wear one of those.' And he was drawing sailing boats.

Dave didn't understand that at all. His grandfather had worked for a car firm in the United States; he was a draughtsman and he used to design cars. He'd gone to America to make his fortune, which he did, then spent all the money and returned home penniless to get married. So Dave could understand that he'd be drawing, but it certainly wouldn't have been boats.

Later in the week, we went to see Dave's mum and told her what had happened. Without a word, she went upstairs and came down with piles of sketches of sailing ships. Her dad had loved ships and had spent all his spare time drawing them. Dave had never seen them.

For Dave, that was wonderful. It was an example of the most convincing type of contact that the medium can make. Dave had no knowledge or recollection whatever of the fact that his grandad drew sailing ships, so I could not have been reading his mind. From being a complete non-believer, he changed instantly to being convinced that there *is* life after death.

By that stage, unlike Dave, I did believe in the afterlife. Shortly after my dad died, I dreamed that he was there with me, and I knew that he really was.

I told Dave, and he just said, 'Yes, love, if you want to think that.' I was infuriated, because I knew that what I'd just experienced was real.

When I started mediumship, Dave said, 'If it keeps you happy, then fine,' and he was always supportive of me. That experience with his grandfather, though, changed his belief forever because it gave him personal proof, beyond a doubt, of the existence of life after death.

Interestingly, I've often found that it's not some profound message that suddenly changes people's attitudes. Just telling them mundane, intimate facts about a person, often unknown to them, which when checked out are found to be correct, gives them concrete proof – and often makes them view life and death in a completely different way.

How did you practise and develop your mediumship?

Within my first development circle the emphasis was on finding and connecting with spirit guides, or helpers. These are highly evolved spirit beings who at times draw close to our consciousness in order to help us on our spiritual journey.

In the circle, the idea was that you need not develop your own mediumship beyond sensing this guide, because the guide would then contact people in the spirit world and tell you who they were and what they were saying. In other words, your guide would do the mediumship for you. So we used to sit around waiting for guides and helpers to appear.

One day, early on, I remember sitting there, and I had a feeling just as if someone had shoved me in the back. I stood up in the room and started dancing. Then I began speaking in someone else's voice. I have no recollection of anything that was said, as I was in a trance state, but apparently it was a woman who spoke very quickly and with a Chinese accent.

Unfortunately, it seemed that whatever I did in that circle was wrong. I had even been told that I would never become a medium! When I came out of trance, the leader of the group said it wasn't a guide and that I was making it all up.

But I knew I wasn't. Over time, it came to the point where I could actually sense her with me. If I asked for help, she would come. I could talk to her in my mind and ask questions and she would answer. So, as far as the development of my mediumship goes, I really have to thank my spirit guide, San Lo, because she was my guide and my best friend and has always been there for me.

San Lo liked to interact with people; she would touch them and hold them. She would fill people so much with the joy of spirit that they would want to dance. She loved people and had no problems showing that love, and they responded to that. Because she was always full of joy and laughter, she raised the energy and got everything going; she affected people and made things happen. She never spoke in an authoritarian manner. In fact she always came across as very humble.

I saw this relationship between San Lo and myself as a very natural thing. My view was always that mediumship was a joyous and uplifting experience. It was something to be enjoyed, and I would like to get it across with an attitude which was humourous and fun rather than heavy or authoritarian.

But when, in later years, I went to the College of Psychic Studies in Stansted, I found that they worked with guides very differently.

At the College, the medium would sit in trance and just talk; there was no excitement or animation or interaction with the audience. I remember one medium had two people sitting beside him holding on to his arms. A woman who had not previously witnessed trance said afterwards, 'Did they have to hold him down?'

So, thinking that my method must be wrong, I put San Lo on one side and didn't work with her for a long time.

Finally, as the song goes, 'I did it my way.' I worked with her as I naturally wanted to. The group I was then working with was just blown away by her.

I've mentioned Gordon Higginson already. He was the President of the Spiritualists' National Union and Principal of the College, and was the first person who really encouraged me. Other people within the SNU supported me, including Joyce Steedman-McDonald, a minister of the Church, who was then involved in the education of trainee mediums within the West Midlands. She is a very caring person, and she suggested I should get my certificate of mediumship, or CSNU. Nora Shaw, from County Durham, who was at that time

Chairman of the Mediumship Education Committee at national level, was also very supportive. She later encouraged me to take the exam for the Tutor of the Spiritualists' National Union, or TSNU, which qualified me to train teachers of mediumship.

The Spiritualist Church at this time wanted people to do exams in order to establish some standard for mediumship. So I did them. But in fact they weren't standardised at all, because the exams were organised in such a way that everyone was assessed by different people – all of whom of course had completely different ideas of what mediumship should be.

Does your mediumship always work when you want it to?

Yes. It's much like putting a light switch on; I can control it by mentally allowing myself to become open to the world of spirit. I think that it's very important for mediums to be in control, because otherwise they go about in life constantly aware of the spirit world, which is not healthy. The physical life is very important. Knowing that spirit is there to help and guide me is wonderful. But I am not what is called a leaky medium, so the light goes on when I need it, and the light goes off when I've finished.

Having said that, there are times when my mediumship works better than others. Mediumship is affected by so many different things: the natural cycle of the body – for men as well as women; weather conditions, such as heaviness and humidity and thunderstorms; and electrical frequencies, voltages, and power lines, all of which make it more difficult.

I find that my own state of mind can usually be overcome once I've tuned in to spirit. In fact some of my best demonstrations have been when I've been quite stressed or angry about something. Once, my friend couldn't drive me to the church so I needed to borrow my son's car to go to a demonstration. He'd gone to Alton Towers with his girlfriend and they were late back. They finally turned up fifteen minutes before I was due to start, half an hour away. On the drive I was saying to myself that it wasn't his fault; he hadn't done it on purpose. When I got there the anger that had been released made the demonstration go like a dream. I was able to transform anger into creative energy.

How do you switch your mediumship on and off?

At the beginning, I was aware of all sorts of things happening around me. I was open, whether psychically or spiritually, a lot of the time. Initially it was mainly psychic information. When I was with people, I would just sense things about them: their feelings, their aches and pains, or problems that they had. I could tell them all about themselves. At first that's very exciting and gives you a great buzz; it's interesting to tell people what you're sensing and to get some feedback as to whether it's accurate.

Then I began attending meetings at my local Spiritualist Church in Sutton Coldfield, about seven miles north of Birmingham in the West Midlands. I started to practise with spirit contacts, and gradually they were happening more and more often. After a few months, I thought, 'This has got to stop.' I became aware that I had to be able to cut off from it. Also, I do have quite a strong logical side, and airy-fairy stuff never appealed to me at all. Mediums are generally seen as off with the fairies, so once it became clear that, like it or not, I too was one, and not wanting to be seen in this way, I realised that I was going to have to be able to close it down.

As my mediumship never received any formal training, I had to learn that myself. So, using the power of my mind, in much the same way that you block out a problem from your mind, I would switch it off.

Sadly, I can't explain how to switch it on. You can only know how it feels to tune in to the spirit world if you have mediumistic ability.

What does it feel like when you're contacting spirit?

The best way of describing it is 'champagne.' It's joyous, exciting, and uplifting, in fact there's only one thing better!

People who are clairvoyant can see the energy of people both in this world and in the spirit world. They see various colours of the energy field, or aura, that surrounds each of us. I am clairvoyant, but I'm mainly clairsentient, which means that when spirits draw close to me, they merge with my auric field. I feel them in my aura and body, so it feels as if someone is stepping into me.

I feel their personality, their emotions, their memories, I even sometimes take on their mannerisms. While it's actually happening, I'm not aware of anything except what I'm experiencing, and then the feeling of elation is second to none.

In comparison, when you're working psychically, with either the conscious or the unconscious mind of a person here on earth, it's somewhere between a glass of Guinness and a rather good Chardonnay. You can travel through the psyche of a living person, and of course some of that can feel very dark and heavy. Working with the transpersonal, or unconscious, aspects of a person's own psyche, the aim is to release negativity or destructive personality traits that are holding people back from fulfilling their full potential. So in psychic work I was battling all the time with this heavy frequency, which was often hard work and quite difficult to do.

Despite that, the fact is that we are also already spiritual beings while here on earth, so when you're touching the spiritual realms of a person here and now you can feel some of the champagne feeling too.

When working with mediumship and doing many demonstrations, it's very important to keep your feet firmly on the ground. People tell you your demonstrations are brilliant, they feel uplifted and excited after them. Your own feeling after contacting spirit is too incredible to describe. So it's easy for the ego to get a bit too big for its boots. You start thinking you walk on water. I then remember the times when it didn't work so well. I used to tell people I walk on water before eight in the morning – then I get up.

I remember two elderly women from the West Coast of Scotland, who used to travel down to the College for workshops. They adored me, although I could hardly understand a word they said because of their heavy Scottish accent.

Sitting having a coffee with them once, I said, 'I'm coming to Scotland, to Kilmarnock.'

One said, disappointed, 'Oh, that's twenty miles from me.'

I said, 'Do you want me to come into your front room, then?'

Later, when I'd finished a demonstration, she said, in that wonderfully expressive way of hers, 'Oh, heavens, you're f***ing good.' But true to their word, they never did come to Kilmarnock. So it was obviously not good enough to travel twenty miles to see!

After a demonstration, it's essential that you ground yourself. It takes a while to wind down afterwards; it's impossible to do anything that requires thinking, so it's best, whatever the time, to do something mindless, sit down and watch TV or do your washing or something – anything which will bring you back down to earth.

Do you have to be in an altered state of consciousness?

Yes. Whenever a medium is working, whether a private sitting or a demonstration, s/he is in an altered state of consciousness. This is a deeply relaxed meditative or trance state different from our normal waking consciousness. Mediumship requires a shift of consciousness, that's why it's always necessary to ground yourself after working, especially if it's been a long night and your consciousness has gone deeper and deeper into that state of trance.

When working with my guide, I was always deeply overshadowed by her personality. After a session with her, the whole of my being was resonating at a higher frequency; it felt as if parts of me were outside of myself. I would therefore have to spend some quiet time afterwards to get back to normal. It's as if the whole of your psyche is unbalanced, quivering – like an underset jelly on a plate which has to be put back into the mould.

Once, while working with San Lo in Sutton Coldfield Church, I was in that deeper state of consciousness. Someone got up to dim the lights, only he turned them up by mistake. I felt it like a kick in the stomach. I grabbed someone's arm. We discovered later that it was covered in bruises.

When you're working, and in an altered state of consciousness, any interruption, the tiniest incident, can have a devastating effect. It's a bit like being woken suddenly from a deep sleep. It can be quite shocking and unpleasant. You're very vulnerable. Things that people say, even quite inadvertently, can hurt tremendously. Also, whenever possible, I would ask someone to drive me to the church, especially if it was a long way away, because it really wouldn't be safe for me to drive back at the end of a night.

What is a spirit?

A spirit is the spark of life that we all have, the life force within us that is us. It's so difficult to define, yet it's what makes life possible. Every living thing contains that life force, whether human beings, plants, animals or insects. When we pass to the other world, the physical body is left behind, but that life force still exists.

For example, there are wonderful photos that show the auric field around leaves. When the leaf is on the tree, its aura is vibrant and full of energy. When the leaf falls from the tree, as it falls you can actually see the life force decreasing within its aura. It is an energy that can be dissipated but cannot be destroyed.

Which truly begs us to respect the whole of life, not just ourselves but the animals and plants and mother earth. We have a responsibility not only to each other, but also to all of life. We must have tolerance of all living things. What we're doing to planet earth is unforgivable. But there are some people who profess to be religious, yet treat plants and animals as if they don't count, and kill them without a thought.

In terms of mediumship, a spirit is someone who has shed the physical overcoat and passed on to the next part of their journey into eternity.

In the spirit world, we are essentially as we are now, but without a physical body. People in the spirit world have the same feelings and memories, their personality traits are still there. They're not all-knowing and all-seeing. They *haven't* grown wings overnight.

On the other hand, pure spirit is different. It is no longer the personality, the feelings and memories. Pure spirit is a pure energy. Whatever we experience in this life, we're always learning, and we travel through many years and even many lifetimes learning, and eventually we go back to that pure form. The God force is always expanding. We are energy, our awareness and consciousness are constantly expanding as we go on our eternal journey towards that God force.

People in the spirit world are not miracle makers, and people often attribute things to spirit which they have actually brought about themselves. A psychic can tell you that something particular is going to happen, and hearing that might push you to get on and do what has been told, but in the end it's you that's doing it. We're all responsible for ourselves; we all have to take responsibility for what we say, do and think throughout our lives.

We all have the opportunity to shed a bit of light just by being, by having an effect on others we meet. When we accept the God force within us, we can look on people more kindly and with more compassion. We become a beacon of light, and people are happier after meeting us.

We have to work through our human personalities, resolve our inner conflicts, and be content in ourselves. The spirit world can't do that for us. It might uplift us and inspire us, but we still have to put the work in and make things right in our world.

If I don't believe in the afterlife, what will happen when I die?

You will still live. You will still be alive, though it may take you some time to accept that. You will not be abandoned, because there will always be people in the spirit world who will try to help you. But, whether you like it or not, you will continue to live.

It is well documented that many people see a loved one in the moments prior to death, even to the extent of shouting out their name. A friend came for a sitting when her uncle was very poorly in hospital. He was well into his seventies, and I said to her, 'He's getting ready to go, his mum's there, waiting for him. It'll be three days.' My friend was with him three days later, in the hospital, when he suddenly regained consciousness. He sat bolt upright, popped in his false teeth, and said, 'There's me mum, she's come for me. I'm coming, Mum,' and at that moment he died.

There is always someone to meet us when we pass over. Friends or family or people we have known will gather round and be ready to meet us on the other side.

Whether we accept them or not is another matter. Some people may not believe that they are dead. It does happen. When they are met by relatives or friends, they say 'You're dead and I'm not.' They can't acknowledge that they are not still in a body.

Each individual has to come to their realisation of the afterlife in their own time. Sometimes their belief systems are so strongly against the continuity of consciousness that even though they are clearly experiencing it for themselves, they cannot accept it. Even in spirit, there are those who still refuse to believe in the spirit world. They may be in a state of stillness (or, if you like, dead) waiting for their messiah or their trumpet to sound, not realising that they have to change within themselves to accept their new way of being.

Someone from another realm will always manifest to help these people, who are so locked into their state of mind that they cannot embrace their new state of being. The amount of work that goes in from the other side of life to relieve these people of their doubts is amazing.

I know that there are loved ones and friends on the other side who try to help in the transformation into this new life, and I believe that our prayers and healing thoughts can also help, especially when people have passed in tragic circumstances.

A lot of people would like death to be the end, often because they've had a difficult or painful life and have not managed to solve their problems or overcome the vast mountains of despair that they carry around with them.

Sometimes we forget that in being human, we have faults; accepting these faults, we can forgive ourselves and others far more easily. But the vast majority of people don't do this. So when they reach the spirit world, they are still grappling with those same problems. They're still struggling to accept themselves as they really are.

A spirit is the energy, memories, thoughts and feelings of a person that continues to exist after the death of that person's physical body. But the key word is continues. We also have a spirit here and now, while we're alive.

Realising this, we're probably going to live our lives a bit differently than we have been doing. Knowing this allows us to make sense of our very humanness.

How has being a medium affected your life?

It's had its ups-and-downs.

I'd like to say it's been a bed of roses, but it hasn't. Which has nothing to do with the spirit world; it's to do with my own self-critical personality, and the clashes with some, but by no means all, of my colleagues who didn't have the same ethics as I did.

And it made me ill. When I was working full-time with mediumship, I worked flat out. (So did many other mediums with whom I worked, and their health was often terrible too.) I was travelling a lot, my eating habits were all over the place, and the cumulative stress eventually led to hypothyroidism. In fact, many mediums are diabetic or have thyroid problems.

Being a medium affected my family life as I was away from home so much. On Sundays I was normally working in a church, which would usually mean leaving home early afternoon and getting back late, so when my children were grown up and working, I would hardly see them. It got so crazy that we'd have to make an appointment to meet!

Three years before I moved to Spain, it was as if I was stuck on a merry-go-round. I felt that I had lost touch with God, and I really needed to step away and feel content again.

The final year that I was working, I was booked to be away from home for twenty-six weeks, and all the time in between was booked up as well. 'Time to stop,' I thought.

So I did. At first I missed it immensely, because my life had been so eventful and hectic, but I soon started painting and reading and playing my clarinet. And then I moved to Spain and started work on this book.

Mediumship has brought me a lot of pain, but it's also brought me a lot of joy, and a tremendous amount of laughter. I just thank God that I have had such a supportive husband and children.

What do you believe is the purpose of life?

For me, it has always been to find out who I am in the scheme of things. I was always questioning, wanting to understand more about life's mysteries. In a sense, I was seeking the spirit both within and without.

We all have a need to work on ourselves, to understand ourselves and to admit to, and take responsibility for, our own feelings. I believe we also all have a need, somewhere deep within, to find God. And to do that, we have to be open.

But that's a choice we each have to make. We can choose to work on ourselves, to learn and to be creative, or we can choose to ignore our own spirit within. The problem is that many people have suffered a great deal of pain and trauma throughout their lives, and they may not feel that there is anything that they can do about it.

I have always had the belief that there is a way out. We can all get out of pain and discover joy. The joy of spirit, and of life itself, is open to everyone. We all have tremendous capabilities of what we can achieve with our minds. The power of thought is amazing and immense. Using that power, we can transform our lives.

We are all constantly evolving. That to me is the purpose of life: to learn about ourselves and the world around us, to learn how we can love, and how we can forgive.

We may say our prayers, we may say we believe in God, yet many of us don't actively work at forgiveness.

The greatest challenge we face is to find within ourselves the divine spark – to find our own unique connection to the source of all life and of all love.

CHAPTER THREE

Myths about Mediumship

Myths concerning mediumship abound. Let's look at a few.

Myth No. 1: A medium is born

In my experience, that's not necessarily the case. What is true, for a variety of reasons, is that many people are more sensitive during childhood than they are as adults. Children are open and receptive and are often adept (and less inhibited) at tuning in to other people's energies and emotions. They may sense spirit and accept this as normal; later, perhaps when they're told that such things don't exist, they begin to doubt their own experience. Our Western belief system tends to view spiritual phenomena with fear or incredulity, therefore in adulthood many people become closed to further experiences of this kind.

Mediumistic ability can begin at any point in life. I was twenty-nine when I first began to sense spirit. Other mediums say that that it has been with them for the whole of their lives.

Myth No. 2: Mediumship can be learned

Mediums can certainly be guided to expand their abilities. Mediumship training can help mediums to understand what they're sensing. It can help them to explain more fully the messages, information or images that they are getting, and to be able to go deeper into the contact so that they can give a better description of the contact, hold it longer and go into more detail. But no, I don't believe that mediumship can be learned.

Myth No. 3: Everything that a medium receives comes from spirit

It's probably true to say that a lot of the information that we receive comes from the psyche of the person we are working with, rather than from the spirit world. Because all mediums are also psychic, they sense things that are coming from the subconscious mind or from the energy field, or aura, of the person with whom they are working.

All of our experiences throughout our lives – events, relationships, joys and sadnesses – become imprinted on our energy system, stored within our unconscious mind or the cells of our body. Therefore a person who is able to tune into the energy field of another person can draw much information about him or her from it. This is why it is so important for a medium to be able to clearly distinguish between information obtained psychically and that coming from the spirit world.

When my mediumship had been established for some years, I started to question whether all that I was sensing was actually from the spirit world. That was when I started to study transpersonal psychology. This originates from the work of the psychologist Carl Jung, which explains the human psyche in terms of individual, spiritual and religious aspects, exploring man's connectedness to himself, his fellow man, to God, and to the whole of life.

Jung believed that there are many different parts of our personality of which we are not consciously aware. He called these sub-personalities. They are aspects of ourselves which, because we have not consciously acknowledged and integrated them, are hidden within our unconscious mind, constituting what he called the Shadow Self.

I realised that at times, rather than working mediumistically, I was in fact working psychically. The spirit world does not communicate in the sort of symbols and images that I was seeing and sensing, which were in fact coming from within people's unconscious mind and were simply representations of their own sub-personalities. I learned to actually feel the difference between the frequencies of the spirit world and the symbols and images of the unconscious mind. Working in this way, I was able to help people to recognise and integrate those sub-personalities consciously, giving them a greater understanding of themselves, their feelings, actions and reactions.

Myth No. 4: A medium only tells you what you already know

If a medium is working mainly at the psychic level, then the information that he or she gives you will be drawn from your unconscious mind. Which means that, in some sense, you already know it, even if you have forgotten it or are not consciously aware of it. For example, a medium working psychically may tell you of fears, hopes and plans that are prominent in your mind. On the other hand, spirit may provide information of which you have no knowledge whatsoever.

Once on the platform I gave the name of a woman in spirit, and details of where she used to live, but it meant nothing to the woman receiving it. She knew nothing about her, so had trouble accepting that the contact was for her. A few days later, however, she rang me, saying that she had asked her mother, and it was someone her mother used to know, a distant relative, whom she herself had never met.

Another time, I had a contact for a woman, and I described an old lady in spirit, giving her full name and the number of the house and the road where she used to live. She was saying she used to come and borrow sugar from the woman's mother. The woman herself had no recollection. So she went to the records office and found that the old lady did indeed live there, during wartime, and had been a neighbour of her mother's.

It's often been very powerful and convincing when I've given people details which at the time they thought were irrelevant, or had nothing to do with the person they knew, and then later they have checked out that information from other sources and found it to be correct. But clearly, if too much of the information contains details of which the person has no knowledge, s/he will find it difficult to relate to that particular contact, and may even feel that I am mistaken when I say that the contact is for them.

Myth No. 5: Mediums are fortune-tellers

Not so. I strongly believe that a medium should resist any urge to tell anyone what's going to happen to them. We don't know what the future holds. Even if we see images of certain events or circumstances, they are merely possibilities, and the person concerned is himself directing the course of his own life. We all make choices, and we all determine whether we will follow one or other of the many paths open to us. The power of suggestion is enormous, and to tell someone that something is going to happen in a certain way undermines both his freedom to choose and his personal responsibility for the choices he makes.

Myth No. 6: Mediums are schizophrenic

The gap between mediumship and psychiatry is not as great as one might imagine. Teresa told me of one study which shows that when a medium is in the same room as a person diagnosed as schizophrenic on account of the 'imaginary' voices he is hearing, in up to 15% of cases the medium is able to hear those same voices and report the same conversations as the person himself is hearing. This should be of great interest to those dealing with mental illness. Unfortunately, to date, the psychiatric community has not shown itself to be tremendously open to such alternative explanations of so-called psychopathological phenomena.

All of us experience pseudo-hallucinations, or products of our own imagination, as we fall asleep (hypnogogic) and when we are waking up (hypnopompic hallucinations). A true hallucination as defined in psychiatry is a sensory perception experienced in the absence of an external stimulus, yet felt to originate outside of us. Which begs the whole question of mediumship, because the medium is experiencing a sensation originating in an external stimulus, i.e. the spirit world, which the majority of people are unable to perceive.

For this reason, probably every medium has at some time doubted his or her own sanity, especially when first working with spirit. It can be very difficult to differentiate between a normal sensation owned by oneself, a shared sensation, i.e. one that is being primarily experienced by another person and being picked up or sensed by the medium, and a sensation originating in spirit. It takes practice to distinguish energetically between them.

The point is that all of us interpret our sensations in the light of our own beliefs. Our minds determine our realities. Madness is defined as a loss of contact with reality – but whose reality?

All of us define – and limit – our own realities. The whole of psychiatric classification hangs on the central issue of the consensus of reality as defined by the society in which we live. Until our social values reflect a greater spiritual dimension, the reality of the spirit world will continue to be held in question. Until we acknowledge that our subconscious minds, our dreams, and the energy systems, both of us as human beings and those of spirit beings, are all coexisting realities similar yet different to our normal waking consciousness, we will find it hard to be fully open to the infinite possibilities of the wonderful and mysterious universe in which we live.

Myth No. 7: Mediumship is harmful

Einstein's theory of relativity was a beautiful, brilliant and original idea. The fact that it provided the theoretical basis for the release of the enormous energy contained within the atom and ultimately to the development of the atomic bomb does not make his work any the less brilliant or beautiful. The use that we make of any of the gifts that we are given is a reflection of us, not of the gift itself and certainly not of the giver of those gifts, whoever we may perceive that to be. Knowledge of any kind is power, and it's up to each of us how we use that power.

Mediumship in its best use can bring faith, hope and comfort to millions of people.

Quite simply, it can change lives in far-reaching and astonishing ways. It is a brilliant, beautiful and unique affirmation of the unity of all creation, not least because it fits very neatly into Einstein's discovery that matter is energy and that energy cannot be created or destroyed.

Mediumship can be misused, through motives of greed, egotism or vanity. But there again, so can everything.

Myth No. 8: Spirits can cause us harm

Spirits are human beings without physical bodies. They therefore exhibit the whole range of human strengths and weaknesses, of qualities and defects. Perhaps some of the problems that arise are linked to the fact that sometimes they have so much difficulty getting through and being heard.

Many of us are frightened or disturbed by the unknown, by occurrences that we cannot readily perceive through our five senses – or that we cannot explain. Quite a number of people who do not consider themselves to be mediumistic can nevertheless sense spirits. Yet they never think to ask those spirits why they are there or what they are seeking. Maybe we react just from our own point of view and don't stop to consider what the spirit needs or what we could do to help. Sometimes a spirit does need help because s/he is trying to get a message through and is unable to do so.

As I've said before, a lot of people when they pass into the spirit world just carry on living the lives that they were living before, causing no harm to anyone. However, if we don't understand this, then we may be frightened or disturbed if we sense them and feel they're intruding on our environment and we don't know why they're there.

There are rare occasions, nonetheless, when we're going to need some specialised help if a spirit is acting in an unusually negative or destructive manner – which leads to the next myth.

Myth No. 9: When we pass into spirit we are suddenly transformed to a higher spiritual level

This is not so. In fact, especially when a person has passed suddenly, it can be hard for that spirit to orientate to that new-found state of bodylessness. His or her consciousness, although suddenly separate and independent of the physical world, may retain strong emotional attachments to the plane of existence that s/he has left behind. This may be particularly the case if that person in human life has strongly believed that life ends with physical death. To suddenly discover whole realms of non-physical existence must certainly come as a bit of a shock! And perhaps as a source of sadness, as the gravity of what s/he has missed out on in life as a result of that belief gradually dawns. As we said earlier, our minds determine our realities. Our beliefs limit our own realities.

One of the main purposes of mediumship in my view is to make people here on earth aware of the continuity of consciousness. There is no ending. There is no sudden elevation to heavenly realms or descent to hellish depths. In fact, it's pretty much business as usual. The emotions, the problems, the learning and insights about ourselves that we had made and the areas in which we were stuck or resistant to change continue to hold us in much the same way as they did when we here on earth. Which explains why sometimes it will take a long time for a spirit being to be able to come through and say the things that s/he needs to say.

Of course, we can't rule out that s/he may have been trying for some time before anyone listens or before someone who can hear is in a position to give that message to the person it's intended for. But also that spirit may have taken some time to get to a point where s/he is able to say those words. Communication from spirit to the human mind is fraught with difficulties.

Often a spirit will be wanting to say; 'I'm sorry I never told you I loved you.' Maybe we can all learn from that. It can be very difficult to say the things we need to say. But telling people what we feel can have a wonderfully healing effect, for them and for us, and sometimes just to say, 'I'm sorry', or 'I love you', makes a world of difference.

That's why I always urge people to do it now, while they have the chance. Don't wait till you're in spirit because then it is much harder to say. Or, rather, it's much harder for it to be heard.

Myth No. 10: Life's a bitch and then you die

It's sometimes said that those who are left are worse off than those who have passed. But that's probably only so if those who are left don't believe in spirit life. Knowing that our consciousness continues to exist, and continues to learn and grow whether or not we have a physical body, means that we should be able to make better use of the time we have on earth. Paradoxically maybe, the knowledge that problems aren't going to go away just because our physical bodies have gone means we might make more of an effort to solve some of those problems here and now rather than imagining that one day we'll be dead so we won't have to bother.

We've all met old – and not so old – people who say, 'I'm never going to change now.' But why not? We can't stop changing, whether we like it or not, and the biggest change of all is yet to be faced, the transition from the physical world to the spirit world. We think that we're going to die when really we're not going to at all. In fact we're going to be still here. Knowing that there is no death (in the sense anyway of a book's end rather than a chapter's), we can get more out of life; we can make the most of our opportunities to love more, to learn more, and to release more of our pain.

Myth No. 11: Mediums go round meddling

A woman in my apartment block said of me to a mutual friend; 'I dread meeting her in the lift in case she reads my mind.'

I've spent over thirty years doing psychic and mediumistic work. I've worked with many hundreds of people, and I can honestly say I've never read anyone's mind in a lift. I close off to the spirit world when I'm getting on with my own life, and even when I am sensing something, I don't tell people unless they want to know.

Mediumship isn't about meddling, it's about facilitating communication. We all have the need to express our feelings, and sometimes we need help with that. Spirits communicate because they have something to say. That's usually only a problem if we don't want to hear it.

Mediumship undoubtedly carries a responsibility. The personality and integrity of the medium determines how he or she will meet that responsibility. My responsibility has always been first and foremost to the spirit world. For me, a medium's job is to give proof of life after death and to help the spirit world.

Myth No. 12: Mediums only talk to dead people

Not so. A medium can receive a communication from a spirit or from a living person. A person might be very ill, unable to speak or comatose, and, while he is ready to pass into spirit, he fears that his loved ones on earth will not be able to cope without him. They may be desperately wanting him to stay or begging him not to go. He may not be able to go until he has received their blessing, yet he cannot ask for it directly.

For example, I was seeing a client, Joy, whose husband was in a coma in hospital. One day their daughter, Kate, came to see me. While we were talking, her father, who was also a medium, communicated to me. He described to me a man he'd met in the spirit world. From that description Kate recognised it as his spirit guide, of whom he had often spoken. Her father said how sorry he was about the things he'd done, and how much he loved Kate. Then he said to her, 'Ask your mum to let me go.'

Joy went that day to see him while he was still unconscious. She said she'd had the message from him and that it was alright to go. In the middle of the night she had a phone call from the ward saying that he had regained consciousness. Joy was amazed, wondering what was going on. She thought he wanted to go home to the spirit world, yet here he was back again. She went to the hospital and they made up, forgave each other for the years they'd wasted, and he died peacefully that night.

A few days later, I was getting ready to go to the funeral when I heard his voice asking me to get some pink carnations for his daughter and some red roses for Joy. After the funeral I gave them the flowers. They both burst into tears because the flowers had special meaning for each of them. He communicated to them both before and after his death, and this enabled them all to forgive and to heal.

Myth No. 13: It's too late

Sometimes when a spirit makes contact with a person and says sorry, that person is too angry and upset to be able to accept that apology. If a person has been abusive and destructive, and has not taken responsibility for his actions during his life, then it can be very difficult for those left behind to believe that he is suddenly able to see his actions in a different light. They may be unable to accept that he is truly sorry. As a result they cannot bring themselves to forgive the damage and hurt that he has caused.

Some people live their lives in a blur without awareness of themselves or the consequences for others of their actions. Negative, demanding, and without compassion, they cannot accept that they have done anything wrong or that they have anything to learn. The fact is that damaged people damage others. And so the cycle goes on. For such people, passing into spirit may be their first true experience of acceptance, joy and unconditional love. It may be the first time they become aware that everything we do has consequences – for ourselves and for others.

To forgive others for the damage they have caused us is probably the hardest challenge we ever face. We have to change and shift our attitudes and look even deeper into our own hearts. However, we are always being given the opportunity to learn and we always have the possibility to love. However much we have been hurt, and whatever bitterness and anger we may have felt, we can all break the cycle of pain and blame – because every single one of us has the capacity to love, and love is the only thing that can ever truly bring a change of heart.

The whole point of mediumship is that never is it too late.

CHAPTER FOUR

What a Medium Does:
Questions and Answers

How did you discover mediumship?

Mediumship reached its peak between the two world wars. After so much loss and suffering, people were in need of spiritual help and desperate for something in which to believe. But it was only in 1951 that it became legal, when the Witchcraft Act was repealed and replaced by the Fraudulent Mediums Act.

Prior to 1951, people had to meet very quietly in private houses. The police would watch the house if they were aware of meetings going on, and mediumship as a result was very much on the fringe and seen as pretty scary.

In fact it must have been scary, sitting around in a house in a circle with the lights low and a man sitting in a trance waiting for spirits to contact him. You wouldn't know what would happen or who might appear. It would have frightened the life out of me.

I grew up amongst a somewhat confusing background of beliefs: an atheist father, a mother who simply believed in the Lord, and a Catholic grandmother who was mediumistic.

My grandmother used to see my grandfather after he'd died, standing by the foot of the bed. She would talk quite openly about it. So I always believed in life after death, although I found it all a bit frightening. My mother was scared and my father thought it was all a load of rubbish. In fact he used to say, 'When I'm dead, have me stuffed and black-leaded, and put me in the hall as a coat-rack!'

From the age of eight till about ten, I went to Sunday school – not that my parents made me go, it was just that I wanted to. But when I got there I was always arguing. For me, if Jesus was the Son of God, then I must be His child too. I couldn't understand why God only had one son. In the same way, when I was told that God would punish me for doing something, I used to think I wouldn't punish my kids that way. What a nasty God to have, that punishes you for being human.

In the 1960s, there were Spiritualist Churches about, but I would never have gone to one. Lots of people wouldn't tell their friends, neighbours, or even their husbands where they were going. They were instilled with the Christian morality which said that anything linked with mediumship was to do with the devil. So in those days – and for many people still today – mediumship was clouded by fear and guilt.

Nowadays, although there is still prejudice against things of the spirit, Christianity has less hold over people. Thirty years ago, however, there was a very different state of mind. Attitudes are slow to change. Even much later, when I'd been involved in mediumship for years, although having the full support of my husband, Dave, and my two children, Kerrie and Stuart, none of my family ever asked what I was doing.

My father died in 1973, when I was twenty-nine, and I was devastated. He was the most honest, kind man you could ever wish to meet, and he expected everyone else to be honest too. He used to buy his shoes from the insurance man, who called every week, and one time he was overcharged by two shillings and sixpence. My dad, straight as a die, wouldn't have anything to do with the man after that. In fact the only time I ever remember him giving me the slipper was after I had told a fib, and he said then that he would forgive me anything but telling lies.

Dad didn't believe in the afterlife, and he was against organised religion, so he never believed in God in the conventional sense. He said that with all the money the Church had, why weren't they doing anything to help the poor?

Occasionally, he and I used to walk with my mother to the Three Crowns pub, which was in the middle of the country towards Walsall, famous for its leather tanneries in the industrial West Midlands. We'd sit in the gardens there having a drink on a summer evening. Once, I remember pulling a branch off a shrub as we walked along one of the lanes, and he said, 'Why are you doing that? Don't you think that the tree can feel that and is in pain?'

Just before Dad's funeral I had a dream in which he and I were walking together around Cannon Hill Park in Birmingham. In the dream he said to me, 'Fancy you thinking I was dead, and I was here all the time.' When I woke up, my hand ached from where I had been holding his hand so tightly.

I know dreams can have different meanings, and to see a loved one in a dream can be simply telling us about ourselves, but that was my dad, I was convinced. I knew it was him, and I felt safe because I knew he was still there.

Up till then I had been scared. But after that dream I knew for sure that the afterlife existed.

About a year later I started taking my mother to a local healer. He used to hold meetings in his house, and one evening he was demonstrating mediumship. I had heard of his mediumistic abilities and, in the hope that he might be able to contact my father, I stayed on.

At that meeting I received a message from my grandmother. The medium told me, 'I've got Polly here and she's told me to tell you she's got her teeth in, and Tilly wants to say hello.' This might seem like a ridiculous message to anyone else, but whenever I used to visit Nan, I'd go into the lounge and say, 'For God's sake, Poll, put your teeth in,' and, laughing, she'd take them out of her pinnie pocket and put them in her mouth.

When I was a child, Nan would meet her friend Tilly down at the pub for a half of Guinness every lunchtime except Sunday. Just one. One day Nan was walking back up the hill when she stopped to catch her breath. She decided to tidy her handbag while waiting to get her breath back. She cleared out a wad of tissues and threw them over the hedge, which happened to be the garden of one of the police houses. When she got home she found she'd lost her teeth and realised that she must have thrown them over the wall. But she was too scared to go and ask for them because it was the policeman's garden, so she never did get those teeth back.

So the message about the teeth was just what I'd expect my Nan to say. Tilly had died when I was ten so, although I wondered whether the medium might just be reading my mind, I hadn't thought of Tilly or even heard her name in over twenty years.

Although I didn't have another message from any of my relatives who'd passed over until twenty-nine years later, the message from my grandmother about Tilly made me think that there was something in this, and my investigations into mediumship started.

I was really excited; it was as if someone had given me the moon. I would look at the stars at night and think how wonderful and immense our universe is. If life after death is true, what other things might also exist too? It brought a sense of joy and excitement into my life, in a way that I had never experienced before. It seemed to open up all sorts of new possibilities and new roads to travel.

At that time, most people of my age were into knitting and house-work, going to the theatre and eating at nice restaurants, and I found it all extremely boring. That mundane stuff never really did anything for me. I was running a shop then, and everyone around me was talking about embroidering and crocheting and recipes and gossip and it struck me that there was more to life than this.

I suppose what I was really looking for was a purpose in life. I hadn't been put on this earth just to clean a house and cook and live a mundane and drab daily routine. My desire to discover more about life after death set me off on a personal journey of self-realisation. Suddenly life had a multitude of new dimensions for me to explore.

I've spent the last thirty years doing just that.

How easy is it to give fine details about a spirit contact?

It isn't easy. It takes a lot of focusing and practice.

Some people aren't prepared to allow their mind to go deeper and deeper into a contact. I remember when I was teaching, there was a student who complained that I wasn't pushing her hard enough, but in fact she simply wasn't taking the advice I was giving.

After one demonstration, she was preening herself a bit. I said, 'If you'd gone a little bit deeper when that lady was talking about her shoes not fitting, you'd have realised that one foot was size six and the other six and a half. She used to work at Cadbury's so those choco-lates she used to bring home were all the chocolate misshapes.'

It's not enough to be satisfied with the first image that comes to mind. Mediums have to continually push their consciousness, not linger too much on descriptions. We need to bring out minute details of what that person liked and what he didn't – the name of his local pub, what drink he used to drink, the type of cigarettes, the fact that his little finger was bent from an old injury. These are the details that leave the person in no doubt that the contact was their father or grandad or whoever.

But the medium has to do the work.

How do spirits usually make themselves known?

How do we normally identify ourselves to people? If we've just met a stranger, we tell them our name, what job we do, perhaps what we're interested in or the things we spend our time doing.

If you were on the phone to someone you used to know well but haven't seen for many years, you'd probably think of some shared memory, something you did together that was funny or unique or that no one else knew about. To an old college friend you might say, 'Remember the time when we skipped lectures and were going to go to Brighton only your car broke down and we made mince pies and ate so many we made ourselves sick?'

If you think about it, if you were in the spirit world and you wanted to talk to your daughter, you wouldn't say, 'Hello, my name was Anne and I lived in Bristol and I had three children.' You'd say, 'Hello love, that clematis outside the back door you always forget to water is looking a bit sorry for itself,' or 'Remember those paint brushes your father always used to leave in a jar of turps on the windowsill in the kitchen?'

The little familiar things we've shared hold the memories of what we were: the moments of laughter or fun, the weird little habits that we all have, the quirks that distinguish us from anybody else.

In spirit our consciousness can project in many different ways; we can project ourselves to a person we used to know in a form in which that person would know us. If a spirit had known someone at the age of twenty, he would appear to that person as a twenty year old. If an elderly person has passed to the spirit world, they can appear as they wish, they might say, 'You've got a photo of me when I was forty…' or appear at a later age. I've decided that when I return from the spirit world, I shall show myself as a twenty-year-old and a size twelve. Problem is, no one will recognise me!

They can tell of their memories, remembering experiences that were shared, how they reacted at the time; perhaps they can now see it differently, and maybe say they were sorry about how they handled things then and have since moved on.

The way I worked with a contact was to say, for example, 'I've got your mother here, and she's telling me she's fine. She's five foot two and she's got white hair and loved M&S clothes.' I'd say what her personality and characteristics were; that she loved cooking, what her favourite dish was, what her house was like, that she liked gardening; then maybe bring back some memories of things they did together.

It's like being at one with the contact, you blend with them to such an extent that it feels as if that person is a part of you. You're stepping into their auric field. It's like putting on a glove. You slip into their way of doing things. Your mannerisms are like theirs. Using clairsentience, that's how it worked for me.

When I was teaching, students would say to a person, 'I've got your mother here,' and then they'd immediately want to rush on and give a message. This could simply come from the psyche of the person in the audience. It could merely be the thoughts or feelings of the person standing in front of you, not from the contact in the spirit world.

I would help the student to go into the mind of the mother, to describe more about her. I would encourage him to take his mind back to the last thing he felt about her; for instance that she had arthritis in her left knee. Taking his mind back to the knee, something else would come into his mind about her. In this way he could deepen his contact and give more and more details that would give absolute proof that it was in fact the person's mother. Then, he could go on and give the message.

We all think of our loved ones when they have passed on. There are concerns and issues and worries that are bound in with our memories of them; there are things we wish they had said. If you had always wanted your father to tell you he was proud of you, then a medium sensing into your auric field will pick up on that emotion as soon as your father is mentioned.

So it's up to the medium to go as far as s/he can into the energy of the spirit s/he is receiving contact from, in order to be sure that what s/he as a medium is relating is beyond doubt originating from the spirit world.

The more you blend with the spirit world, the more you recognise their energy, otherwise you can't distinguish between the spirit world and the psyche of the people here.

Are some spirits difficult to contact?

Yes, and for a variety of reasons. It could be the beliefs they hold or their personality type. If their religious belief is, for example, that it is a sin to communicate with the spirit world, then even when they are on the other side, they may still hold on to that belief.

Many years ago a lady came to me for a reading. The communication was proceeding well when suddenly I became aware of a priest in the background. He wore heavy glasses and he was waving his arms across himself as if to say, 'No way!'

When I described this man, the woman said immediately, 'Oh, that's Father Peter, he died just two weeks ago. He was a wonderful man. I was so hoping that he would talk to me.'

Well, Father Peter still held on to his strong belief system, and would not draw any closer to me. But at least we knew that he had arrived safe and sound. Who knows, maybe one day he will change his mind.

On another occasion I was taking a service in Longton Church, which had been Gordon Higginson's church, the medium I talked about earlier. It was in The Potteries, close to Stoke-on-Trent in Staffordshire. The church, incidentally, was about to be rebuilt on another site. The energy in the new church was never as strong. I suspect because Gordon had passed to the higher life before it was built.

Anyway, in the old church, the platform was like a little theatre, with wings on either side.

The communications were going quite well. I was aware, though, of a lady standing in the wings, peeping out occasionally. She was obviously very timid and afraid of talking in public. As my mind was tuning in and talking to the other people queuing up to have their turn to speak to their loved ones in the congregation, I kept sending reassuring messages to the lady hiding in the wings. It seemed to take forever, but eventually she drew closer into my auric field. Finally, I was able to reunite her with her daughter in the congregation. She confirmed that her mother would not say boo to a goose. She had been shy when she lived on earth and was at this stage of her journey still as shy. She did really well to overcome it, though, and once she had relaxed into my mind she ended up being an excellent communicator.

Are there times when the medium gets it wrong?

Of course. I used to use the analogy of a searchlight: the mind, reaching out to contact the spirit world, is like a searchlight looking for a plane, only there are lots of planes about. So the medium can sometimes pick up a spirit who's not related to anyone in the audience. That can happen when the medium is not completely relaxed, or when the energy is low; his or her mind closes up and it's more difficult to make the contact.

Mediums often give excuses when a demonstration has gone badly, but I believe it's largely to do with us. Mediumship is not an exact science, so although some demonstrations go extremely well, you can do one a few days later and you're struggling. That's what should keep your feet on the ground and stop your ego running away with itself.

Whenever I asked one student how her demonstration had gone, she would always say, 'Oh, everyone said it was brilliant, it went brilliantly.' I wished I could say the same about mine! The point is that if we are constantly looking to work harder for those in the spirit world, we can't sit back on our laurels. We have a responsibility to the unseen world; we are their mouthpiece, and if we don't put the work in, we can't do proper justice to them.

I believe that mediums need to continually analyse the work that they've done, to find out where their mind was going, where they were making mistakes. There are lots of times when the medium has to apologise to the spirit world for not getting it right.

If there's any doubt about a contact, it's up to the medium to make it absolutely clear who the contact actually is, what they're like, what they used to do when they were here on earth. It's too easy to be satisfied with information from the psyche of the bereaved person in front of you, and it's too easy to make assumptions.

At Sutton Coldfield Church there was an elderly man whose name was Les, who frequently came to the demonstrations. Often the medium would say to him, 'I've got a message from your mother.'

'I hope not,' Les would say, 'she's ninety-five and sitting at home in the best of health.'

Based on the fact that Les was seventy-odd, the mediums were simply assuming that his mother would be dead.

Les was utterly convinced of the afterlife. He got us to promise that when he died we'd all sing, 'Wish me Luck as you Wave me Goodbye,' and wave a handkerchief as the coffin went by. When he did die, we all stood there waving and singing. The undertakers looked at us as if we were a bunch of crazies.

Are there people who try to make it difficult for the medium?

Yes! Some of them are totally sceptical. They're testing you, and they don't want things to run smoothly. Working with mediumship, it helps if the audience or the recipient adds in their energy to the communication. Demonstration in public is always touch and go. We used to say that there were times when the atmosphere was just right, the public were on our side and those in spirit were keen to join in; it was like a warm knife cutting through butter. Then there were other times when the audience were not very responsive, the communicators in spirit were just as bad, and it was all so difficult it was like plaiting fog.

I was working in a church in the Leeds area, and the communicator in spirit was more than happy to talk to a man in the congregation. This man was a Minister of the Spiritualists' National Union, but rather than accept what the poor man in spirit was trying to say to him, he was intent on making it as difficult as he could. My memory tells me he used to make life as difficult as he could for everyone on earth too. He sat with his arms crossed over his chest, and every piece of evidence I gave about the man who was trying to talk was met with, 'That is correct.'

After a while, I was so fed up with his attitude, Minister or not, that I declared it felt as if I were sitting an exam. The congregation enjoyed that. I then went on to say that the communicator had a limp.

'Not a bad one,' he retorted.

'Did I say that it was?' I said. The congregation was delighted, as no one had ever spoken to him like that before. My anger fuelled my energy, the audience relaxed and were on my side. After that the demonstration went marvellously.

Is it easier for a medium to contact a spirit for you if you believe in the afterlife?

If your mind is open to the existence of the spirit world, it's easier for the medium to work, whereas if you don't believe in it, and your mind is closed, it can create a barrier which can be difficult for the medium to work through. If the person in the spirit world also doesn't believe in it, or doesn't blend easily with the medium's mind, it's even more difficult.

I always used to tell people who were coming for a private sitting to spend some time in the days preceding the sitting thinking about the person they wanted to contact. Just sending out some thoughts to that person, saying, 'I'm going to see a medium and I'd like you to be there when I do, so that I can talk to you.' Once, when I opened the door to a client, her mother walked in with her. She'd asked her mother to be there, and she was.

Often people were nervous when they came for a sitting, and then I'd always spend some time just chatting to help them relax, because it all works so much more easily when people are open and receptive rather than anxious or suspicious.

There are people who want to test you. They think that you should be able to do it all, and they aren't willing to help in the process. Or they think it will not be genuine if they get involved and ask the spirit to be around. There are others who expect the medium to furnish information to the nth degree, and whatever you give they'll be disappointed. On a few occasions it was impossible to make any contact. The person was so closed, aggressive even, that I was unable to get anything at all. But that was rare.

Most people who come to a sitting or a demonstration are at least open to the possibility of the afterlife. Even if they are sceptical, or their logical mind tells them that it's not possible, that belief changes spontaneously once they've experienced a contact for themselves.

It's marvellous when you're able to give evidence that convinces someone that there really is life after death. Many years ago I used to breed Siamese and Burmese cats, and one of my cat breeding friends asked if I would go to her home town of Burton-on-Trent, a brewing town in Derbyshire, and home of the famous Marmite. Her mother's next-door neighbour had just been discharged from hospital after treatment for cancer, and was asking for some spiritual healing. Her name was Shirley, and she was a really lovely lady. Together with a healer friend of mine, I made several trips to see her.

After a while, Shirley was a lot stronger and once a week for the next eighteen months her husband would drive the thirty miles to bring her to my home for healing. A non-believer, he would never come into the house but sat outside in the car reading a book.

Shirley was smallish with mousy hair and would often wear a twin set and pearls, a typical middle-aged woman of a middle-class background. She told me that in her earlier years she had been a Sunday school teacher, and she very much looked the part.

During one particular session, the healing energy was particularly powerful, but at the same time extremely peaceful. The whole room seemed to shimmer.

It was then that I became aware of the figure of Jesus standing in front of Shirley. Tears were running down my cheeks. The atmosphere was so beautiful, it really was amazing. After I had finished the healing, I stepped back from the chair. Shirley's back was towards me. It often took her quite a while to become aware of her surroundings again, but this time it took longer than usual.

When she turned to me, there were tears running down both her cheeks.

'I kissed the hem of His gown,' she said, as soon as she looked at me. She too had witnessed the echo of Jesus standing before her.

Shirley knew that her time on this earth would not be long. The healing helped her to cope with the illness, and she said that it brought serenity into her days. A couple of weeks before she died, she asked her husband to take her to their cottage in the Lowlands of her native Scotland. The journey was arduous but she was determined to return home in order to meet her Maker. The end was peaceful, in a place that she loved, surrounded by those who loved her.

Several months later, her husband phoned to ask if he could come and see me. Of course he was more than welcome. We chatted, and he cried and shared his grief. Within a short time, we were joined by Shirley. Silly as it sounds I had quite forgotten her lovely, gentle Scottish burr. It was definitely her.

One thing puzzled me, though, because the Shirley I knew was mousy and wore twin set and pearls. Yet now I was hearing her voice but I was seeing a Marilyn Monroe double. When I told her husband, he couldn't believe it.

'That's how she was when I met her! She even wore a white dress like Marilyn.'

A far cry from the middle-aged Shirley I had known, but what wonderful proof for her non-believer husband. Shirley was fine; she was young and healthy and glamorous. And her husband, no longer a non-believer, went away happy in the knowledge that he would meet his wife again.

For all of us, it was an absolutely wonderful experience.

Can you see into the future?

Yes, sometimes, though I don't believe this is my mediumship working. It's my psychic ability.

I always used to say, I don't tell fortunes. Sometimes in a reading I would see a particular event, but in the end the outcome would depend on the person's own choices, and the changes that s/he was prepared to make.

For all of us, a possibility only becomes a reality if we do something to make it happen. If you don't do anything, then nothing is going to happen. Psychic work can empower people to overcome their pains and anxieties. It can show them ways in which they can start making shifts in their perceptions of themselves and their lives, and can help them to integrate aspects of themselves that have been lost or hidden. Simply telling people what is going to happen is taking their power away, and I don't think anyone has the right to do that to another human being.

Mediumship is not intended to tell your fortune or quick-fix your problems. I was always very reluctant to say or do anything that would undermine people's capacity to make their own decisions and choices. I never had a magic wand; the ills of the world would not exist if we did. For all of us, the reality is that we have to change our way of being ourselves, in order to become what we want to be.

In any case, the measurement of time is man-made. The theory of the eternal now explains that the past, the present, and the future are all existing at the same time. So we can access any of those different times right now. Some people reading this book will know exactly what I mean; there have been occasions when they've had a blinding flash and just suddenly, clearly known that something was going to happen. And it did.

We use so little of our minds most of the time. Yet the mind is certainly capable of travelling through so-called time and space. Several books have reported that the Russians and the Americans used psychic mind travel, or remote viewing, to spy on each other.

I never put seeing the future down as one of my fortes, but on the occasions when it has happened, it does seem to have been very accurate. I just wish it had happened for me more often! Or that I had taken more notice of it when it did.

When I first started out within the SNU, I was at home sweeping the back patio one day, and I suddenly got a premonition. It was saying 'beware,' because I was in the same situation as in the first development group I attended. I was going to be betrayed by someone, a woman in the SNU – just as I had been betrayed by a close friend in the development group. It told me that I shouldn't be working with the SNU any more. It hit me like a thunderbolt. But I completely ignored it. I've regretted it ever since.

On another occasion, when the children were small, we were travelling through France along a winding road. There was no traffic, and we were travelling at a reasonable speed. But as we approached the next bend, I suddenly said, 'Stop now!' Dave, a bit nonplussed, pulled over to the side of the road. Thank God I did respond that time because, a moment later, a tractor came round the bend in the middle of the road. If I'd ignored it and we'd carried on, the whole family would have become a message from the spirit world.

And it's not always negative events that we can sense.

While I was doing the transpersonal training, I remember a picture came clearly into my mind. I was travelling in a car on a hilly road. The car was initially old and battered, with children and geese sticking out of the back. Then it changed into a green Porsche. Dave and I were alone in the Porsche, travelling higher and higher into the mists of the mountains, and the car came off the road, fell down the mountainside, yet amazingly neither of us were injured.

I never told Dave about what I'd experienced, but, some years later, I looked out of the window. There was a green Porsche that he had bought me for a present.

About three years later I stopped working. I was disillusioned. It was as if my spiritual journey had come to a halt; I felt the need to find God again. Which is what the images had been telling me all those years before. I just hadn't listened to them.

So, things that have been in our psyche some time before, can come into being.

People reading this will be aware of similar experiences. The problem is that we spend a lot of life swimming against the tide. We're all doing certain things that, deep down, we know aren't right. We carry on doing them because we're afraid to stop. We spend ages being afraid of change, yet when we do finally get round to it, we feel a lot better. Then we wonder why we didn't do it before.

It's always best to listen to the intuitive self; it's part of ourselves that we don't pay much attention to. It's there to protect us, to guide us. I know that I for one have made many mistakes by just not listening enough.

Do you always tell the truth?

I would always tell the truth as much as I could, and tell the truth as I saw it.

I'm naturally a very optimistic person. I don't look for problems so I generally word things in a positive fashion.

Many people who have been bereaved and are seeking help are at a crisis point in their lives; they're lonely and vulnerable and in distress, so it's vital that the medium shows sensitivity and compassion and has a positive outlook and approach to life.

I believe that we all have the opportunity to change and influence the course of our own destiny, so that even if I became aware that some difficulties might arise for a person, I would express that in a way that supported them, and encouraged them to believe in their own capacities to deal with whatever those problems might be.

In a sitting, I could sometimes sense that someone the person knew was going to pass to the spirit world. Then I would be very careful how I put that across. For instance, I was once aware that a man's brother was going to die. But I wouldn't dream of saying, 'Your brother's going to die.'

I could see the man's father in the spirit world and I knew that he was getting ready to meet the brother. In fact, the brother was already ill and I could sense that the man had a concern that he might die. So I said to him, 'I know your brother isn't very well, but don't have any worries because, when his time eventually comes, your father is there in the spirit world and he will be there to meet him, which will make it an easy passage for him.'

What have you learned from mediumship?

Years ago, a psychologist used to come quite frequently for sittings. On one occasion, I was working with the spirit world and I became aware of a magician, a Merlin look-alike. I was just about to say, 'I have a guide here from the spirit world,' when I realised the vibration I was sensing wasn't from the spirit world at all; I was working with her subconscious mind. The magician I had sensed was an aspect of her, a personification of the transformational energy within her own psyche; it had nothing to do with the spirit world.

In the session, I worked with the symbol of the magician and was able to follow Merlin within her psyche. She obviously listened to what he was showing her because, not long afterwards, she left an unhappy marriage, started a relationship with a man much younger than herself, and opened a healing therapy centre. So that was quite a learning experience for me. Realising that there are many different levels of consciousness helped me to work more honestly with the spirit world.

Once, doing a counselling course, we were asked if there was anything that we might hear from a client that would make it impossible for us to feel compassion for that person. For example, we were asked to consider how we would respond if we had a paedophile as a client. To be honest, I found it hard to imagine how I would be compassionate rather than angry in those circumstances.

Then one day I had a client for a private sitting, and I saw in his auric field that he had abused his son. My first reaction was, 'This is gross,' but then I went beyond it and saw what a lonely, abused child he'd been. I could actually touch his spirit, and I thought, 'Yes, I could forgive him for this.' He ended up going to prison. Whether he could forgive himself is another matter.

But for me it was an important moment. It made me realise that whatever we have done, we are still redeemable. Knowing that he had been abused himself, I could see how he could repeat that abuse, and my thinking mind could understand that. But this went beyond normal thinking. I could actually feel the energy of his spirit and it was as wonderful as any discarnate spirit; touching that point of light within him brought a feeling of total elation and joy.

So I learned a lot about compassion from that experience.

In fact, all the sittings I've done have helped me to understand others better, to be less judgemental and to work with more honesty and openness. Mediumship has helped me to expand my awareness of myself and others, and it has also brought me an immense amount of joy. There were so many occasions when the joy of spirit was so strong that I felt I was truly blessed to be able to be a part of that experience. There were some times when, after a sitting, I'd say to Dave, 'If I ever lose my faith about life after death, say this name to me, will you, and it'll remind me of how wonderful that contact was.'

The one contact I had difficulty in accepting, at first, was Princess Diana. The book *Divine Intervention* by Hazel Courteney tells the whole story. Hazel, who is an alternative health writer and was at that time with the *Sunday Times*, had been a client of mine for some years. She had a home in Birmingham as well as in London and, although I would often see her in the Midlands, I'd also sometimes travel to her London home.

I was working at the College one day when I had a phone call asking if I would go and see her. I went to her home in Knightsbridge. After lunch, while walking in Hyde Park, she told me that she had been in contact with Princess Diana. It had started some months before. At first she had no idea what was happening and it had thrown her into complete turmoil. I could see that it was having a devastating effect on her health and her life.

Hazel told me that for months she had been desperate for verification. When she asked Diana to make contact, all she could hear was, 'Call Susan, call Susan.' At first, she couldn't think who Susan was, then it clicked that it was me.

At first, it all sounded so bizarre. But then, when we went back to her mews cottage, as we walked through the door, there was Diana in front of me. Although I'm usually mainly clairsentient, I could see her as plain as could be and she spoke to me.

Hazel and I sat down in the lounge and, as I told her what Diana was saying to me, she said, 'That's exactly what she has said to me.' She was immensely relieved, as there had been times when she'd doubted her own sanity. At the end of the message I said to Hazel, 'It was your experience. My job is to back up what you said and to confirm that it did happen.'

I was sworn to secrecy until the book that Hazel had been writing about her experiences with Diana came out, some twelve months later. When it did, many of my colleagues were extremely cynical about the whole story. But I knew that Hazel was telling the truth. She already had a wonderful lifestyle, was married to a lovely man, and her career was successful, so what could she possibly gain by making up such a story? During the time that Diana had been contacting her, she had become very ill. She couldn't eat or sleep, her husband was worried to death about her, and she'd finally had to give up her job. Who would put themselves through that?

Hazel had sensed Diana. It was a real experience. Before that, she'd never been aware that she was mediumistic. When she suddenly became clairsentient, she didn't know what was happening and, because she didn't know how to let go with the mind, she just went deeper and deeper into Diana's auric field. That's why it had affected her health so much. She simply couldn't close off.

Diana was a woman with great compassion. She had human faults, of course, but no one can take that compassion away from her. Hazel is also a very compassionate and giving person. She had met Diana on a number of occasions, so maybe Diana had recognised within Hazel qualities that she had within herself, and therefore found it easy to blend with her.

Diana's message was that we have to be kind to each other, we have to help each other, and we must look at what we're doing to the earth and start to look after it better. Many people did adore her, so maybe she thought that if she got this message across it would make some impact. But it didn't work: we still kill each other, hate each other and forget all the starving and needy children whom she always tried so hard to help.

At the time of her death, many people believed that Diana had been murdered. I have to repeat what she said to me: that it was an accident, that she was not murdered. She also told me about the inner council that ruled Britain, and that all countries had similar councils, made up of military men and big businessmen. They made most of the governments' decisions. I must admit it sounded like a scary novel.

In fact, the whole thing was just amazing.

Another thing I've learned from mediumship is not to trust what the press say. These days, I don't believe anything that's written in the papers.

For instance, I once did a sitting for Sarah Ferguson, the Duchess of York. At that time the press were always slating her. She was constantly reading in the papers what a terrible person she was supposed to be. I found her friendly and kind; she was truly human, and even made her own cup of tea! But what amazed me were the wonderful colours in her auric field. She has real compassion and truly wants to help people. The press, though, were slaughtering her.

The point is that newspapers can make or break someone. They put people on pedestals, and then, when those people make a mistake, they shoot them down. We buy these papers packed with rumours and lies just because they make a good story, then we judge people on what we read, whether or not it's actually true.

I used to have quite a few people come for sittings from the local TV station. One day, the editor of a news programme came to see me. She said, 'What kind of a person am I turning into? I've just heard there was a crash on the M6 and my first thought was, "How many were injured, will it make a lead story?" I don't know what's happening to me.'

One of the best lessons I've learned in life is to try not to judge. Everyone comes from a different place and there is so much that we just don't know. We've not walked in anyone else's shoes, so how can we judge them? Sometimes it is very hard not to judge others, especially those who affect us personally, but we should all try to show compassion, not least because carrying around hatred and bitterness about others makes it very unlikely that we will ever feel our own joy in life.

What are the most common messages that you have been asked to give from spirit?

Obviously every message is different but the one that seemed to pop up at regular intervals was, 'I'm sorry.' Often the person in spirit simply wanted to say sorry that he – and I say this because it was usually a man – hadn't actually told his wife or girlfriend that he loved her. Although she may have known that he loved her, the words themselves were never spoken.

I remember some time after a friend died, his wife said to me, 'I wonder if he knew I loved him.' Too many of us just don't say those words often enough.

So the most common message was certainly, 'I'm sorry.' Which makes me think that we really need to evaluate the things we've done. We have to apologise, forget our pride, admit our mistakes, and say that we're sorry for our behaviour or our angry words. Otherwise we too will have those regrets when we get to the spirit world. It's much harder to say things when we're over there.

Many people weren't able to say sorry at the time. When, sometimes years later, they appear in spirit wanting to apologise, it occasionally happens that the recipient, too angry to accept it, will say, 'It's too late now.'

But for many it's a wonderful moment: healing and forgiveness are brought about, as well as the person receiving the message also being convinced of life after death.

The one thing I've learned above all others, through working with the spirit world, is to look honestly at myself and be aware of my own behaviour – which has been quite volatile in the past. This means trying to become the observer in any situation, looking at things that are causing me problems, and taking responsibility for my actions.

Once we recognise that being human we all make mistakes, we can see that we're actually sometimes quite cruel in the things we say and do. Having acknowledged that within ourselves, we can start to understand others more clearly, recognise where they're coming from and not be so judgmental. It's when we close our eyes to our own faults that we constantly criticise and see faults in others, and just end up giving more energy to the negativity that exists within all humanity.

It's important to recognise our faults, forgive ourselves, and be able to verbalise our regret to those concerned. If we do that, we no longer have to blame others or feel guilty. And simply admitting our mistakes helps us to be more content within ourselves, which helps us to feel closer to the God force. It helps us to be more caring people. Which is what, in their different ways, most of the world religions talk about.

In terms of other common messages, many people in the spirit world will simply give what appear to be mundane messages. A spirit might say, for instance, 'You've been decorating the lounge then, and put that new paper on all crooked,' and that's simply his way of saying he's interested in what's going on. He can't rehang the paper or make things better, he just talks to his wife in that old familiar way and lets her know that he's still around.

Have you received messages in a different language?

Yes. I was in Italy, for example, working through a translator with a Swiss woman when a gentleman drew close into my consciousness. Being clairsentient, and feeling him so strongly, I was aware that I had to stand up, click my heels together and kiss the woman's hand – which was apparently what he used to do. He then spoke for some considerable time saying many things, all of which were confirmed by her. There were tears and, afterwards, she told me that it was her Russian lover.

Well, I can't speak Russian and he couldn't speak English, yet the thoughts I was getting were in perfect English!

During the course of my mediumship I've had contact with spirits of all nationalities, beliefs, cultures and creeds. I've worked with groups from all over the world including several groups of Norwegians, but the spirit world has never had any problem in communicating to me in English.

The spirit world is capable of overcoming many obstacles. Time, space, and language are certainly no barrier.

Have you seen animals in the spirit world?

I remember being very indignant years ago when I was told by a medium that if an animal had been touched by human love then it could live on in the spirit world. I wondered why humans were so special that their approval could confer immortality!

What happened to the animals that had not been loved, but abused by man? Did a cat that had been so cruelly treated that he had to be put down, or a wild animal that had been hunted and killed, not go to the spirit world? If a piece of fillet steak had been loved did that mean the animal it came from had made it to the after-life?

Some people's attitudes towards animals are quite extraordinary. For example, in the UK it is still illegal to give healing to an animal. Yet who can say that we shouldn't give an animal love? In fact animals are very receptive to healing and they often enjoy it; I know of many that have been saved in this way. I've certainly had tremendous success with cats; if you just put your hand on a cat and send it positive thoughts and healing energy it works very well. I'm sure that anybody with a real love of animals can do it.

I once took in a cat that was being kept outside in a cardboard box. Someone told me about it so I went round and stole it out of the box. He was a silver-tipped chinchilla who we decided to call Zak. He was in a very poor state and had terrible problems with constipation. I decided to give him some colour healing, so I sat with him on my lap and started sending it to him. Just then Dave came in, and I asked him to give the cat a blast of orange too. It didn't work on the cat, he didn't go at all, but I was rushing to the loo all the next day.

Just after that I did a charity event for the People's Dispensary for Sick Animals, the PDSA. There was a cat that lived up the road that had never been in the church before. The door was open, the fluffy grey cat walked in and sat for the whole of the demonstration with its tail right up in the air. Then when I'd finished he got up and went out again.

I was demonstrating mediumship in a local church some years ago when I suddenly saw a big dog from spirit. He was sitting in the aisle by the side of a lady. Then he bounded up the aisle onto the platform and nearly knocked me over. I felt his paws on my shoulders and his tongue washed up my face – which I really hate! When I explained what had happened the lady at the back burst into tears. Her beloved St Bernard had been put to sleep just a few days before. Yet here he was, sitting by her side and welcoming me in exactly the same way as he used to welcome people when he was alive.

I have seen chickens, horses, dogs, ponies, cats, parrots, and canaries in spirit. In a demonstration in Spain many years ago, I had a lady in spirit speaking to me who wanted to talk to Dr Lindy Jordan, who is very well known on the Costa del Sol. I described the lady to Lindy, and she said that it could have been one of two aunts. 'Tell her I have my canary with me,' was the answer, and I saw this bird in its cage.

Lindy said, 'My God, I know which one it is, she took that bloody bird everywhere with her. Even if she was coming to tea, the bird had to come with her.'

How appropriate that she had brought her bird with her once again to say hello to her niece!

I have had cats since I was a child and, many years later, after all the waifs and strays had died, we had Burmese and Siamese cats. Misty, our beautiful lilac queen, died when she was about twelve. It was in May and I had just returned from working abroad. My daughter said how poorly Misty had been, but she perked up for a few hours when I got back. By the evening I knew the time had come for her to go mouse hunting in the sky. There were tears rolling down my face, my husband's too, as I held her while the vet gave her the injections and she closed her eyes and went peacefully to sleep.

At Christmas-time, Dave brought two cups of coffee into the lounge. Placing mine on the coffee table, he turned a little to see where he was about to sit and jumped in the air, spilling his coffee every-where. 'I nearly sat on Misty,' he said. He saw her curled up and asleep on the sofa. He was overjoyed, as he'd never experienced anything like that before.

A few days later he was not so sure, and by the end of the week he was convinced he hadn't really seen her at all! Sadly, that often happens when people in spirit are seen too. Many people say, 'It must just be my imagination.' Well, I hope I don't end up being thought of as imagination when someone sees me after I've gone.

Back in the UK, I often used to see Misty. She'd jump on the bed and walk up between us as she did early every morning when she was demanding that we get up and feed her. I have never seen any of my Siamese cats, though – maybe because Misty, although much smaller than them, was always the gaffer. Anyway, I hope she can find me in Spain!

A medium that came to my local church told me that her beloved chocolate Burmese had recently been shot in the woods behind her home. She was very upset at losing her. She knew I bred Burmese, so we had a long chat. I mentioned that one of my cats was due a litter in two weeks. She said, 'Oh, that's too soon,' then added, 'But will you phone when she has the next litter?' Misty had seven males and one female, and the woman came to look at them when they were about four weeks old. At that point they were all the same size and they all looked exactly the same. She held her hand over each of them and said immediately, 'This is the one.' It was the only female. When she eventually took her home, she bought some new toys for her and also put out some of the old toys. The cat went straight to the old ones and totally ignored the new ones; she then went upstairs, walked along a ledge across the stairs and knocked all the ornaments off, which was exactly the same as the old cat used to do! The woman was absolutely convinced that it was her old cat reincarnated.

A friend of mine had bought a couple of Burmans from a breeder in the Black Country in the West Midlands. She'd also had a litter of Chinchillas. The runt of the litter had been very poorly, it had been touch-and-go whether he would survive. He had problems with his left eye and they thought he was going to lose the sight in it. But it was a gorgeous little cat. He would have nothing to do with anyone except the breeder's husband, whom he adored. When I walked into the house this little cat came running up to me. As I was sitting there, he rolled on his back across my chest, purring like mad, and stayed with me all evening. They couldn't believe it because he never did this with anyone. As soon as I saw him I was convinced that it was Zak who had come back because he used to do exactly the same thing and, in the last year of his life, he had lost his left eye. He'd died the year before; we found him one morning curled up under a tree. So I really felt that this little kitten was Zak. Every time I went to see him I had the same response from him.

So, from my own personal experiences, I can reassure you that when we get to the other side we will have all the wonderful creatures that exist on earth still around us.

CHAPTER FIVE

Developing Mediumship

After that first message from my grandmother, I was convinced that there was life after death. The idea that we all continue to exist after our physical death seemed to make complete sense. But at the same time it made me start to question many of the things going on around me. I wasn't prepared to take things at face value. I had to find out for myself.

Shortly after that message, I began attending the circle regularly. A circle is a group of people who come together to develop their mediumship. We would meet each week; mediums who were already able to contact spirit, and other people who were hoping to. We would have talks and demonstrations. Otherwise we'd basically sit and wait to see what happened.

The idea was that those who could sense spirit would be able to encourage and guide those who were just starting out. By sharing experiences and having some sort of reality check, we would learn better how to discriminate between our own thoughts and emotions and those we were actually receiving from the spirit world.

At least, that was the theory. Of course, it didn't work out like that. As is the case with so many things, rules and egos and power struggles got in the way. It became apparent from an early stage that I was mediumistic and, as my mediumship got stronger, so too did the envy and negativity from others in the group. For me, mediumship was a struggle from the very beginning.

I remember on one occasion, I had a contact for a woman that went very well. She came back to the group the following week to say how wonderful she'd felt and what a moving experience it had been for her. After that I was banned from working in the group for the next six months!

Those first years were hard. It was all new to me and, like many others, I put the established mediums on a pedestal. Of course, they were quite happy to stay there whether or not what they were saying was actually true. But they were the only people I knew who were interested in mediumship, so for a long time I believed what they said.

Looking back, I can see that they saw me not as an ally but as a threat. They wanted everyone to practise mediumship according to their rules. But I was curious and wanted to experiment. The rebel part of me didn't like to be told there was only one way of doing anything.

I started to seriously question what they were teaching when they said that the leader's guide was protecting us all and that if we tried to practise outside of the group we'd attract unwanted spirits. I couldn't believe that the leader was the only one who could ask for protection or help from the spirit world! So, when he was on holiday for a month, I held a meeting at my own home and it went fine. But when I went to their next group, as I walked in, the leader's wife said to me, 'I can see all the stray spirits hanging around you.'

I was banned for a month. I was told that I was too selfish, I wasn't compassionate enough, and that I would never be a medium. Being naïve, I believed it.

I was part of that home group for about ten years. They'd always warned us about going to the Spiritualist Church and, trusting them, I'd kept away. Finally, though, I decided to go. My first venture into a new approach was at Tamworth Spiritualist Church in Staffordshire. I later went to the Spiritualist Church at Sutton Coldfield. I continued to be part of both for the next fourteen years.

For the first few months there, they too were testing me. My mediumship was already developed by then. The view of some members of the committee was that a new member had no right to be a developed medium. But there were some good mediums there, so I stayed. About this time, the Spiritualists' National Union started a training group and I went along with a gang of others to join the group. Everyone was accepted except me.

The man running the group said, 'I can't have you, I'll never be able to control you.' Well, by this stage I was pretty sure I didn't want to be controlled by him or anyone else!

I was never keen on sticking to a set of rules. Instead, I was always looking within myself for ways to improve. I was never satisfied with my mediumship. To me, mediums have to question everything they receive. They have to be continually finding out how they can be of more service to the spirit world. In the end I came to accept that you always make mistakes. Which didn't stop me from constantly looking for perfection. It was engrained in me, to be honest – I learned that from my dad. It was important to me to find out for myself what was true.

So I persevered, began working on platform, and started to gain a reputation as a medium.

One day, when I'd been at Sutton Coldfield Church for about two years, I was at home vacuuming when I heard a voice as clear as a bell saying, 'We want you for teaching.'

'You've got to be joking,' was my response.

Three months later the first awareness group started at the church. I had never led a group before, and we were all surprised when eighty people turned up. The course ran for fifty weeks. Over this time, the numbers dwindled to twenty-five but I carried on teaching the classes, along with other mediums, for the next five years. During this time I also trained to teach meditation and taught classes for the Birmingham Leisure Department.

Then I went to do a course at the Arthur Findlay College for Psychic Studies in Stansted, Essex, where I met Gordon Higginson. He was a man who devoted his life to spiritualism and mediumship. He was one of the best mediums I have ever known. He was the President of Longton Church, which was then known as the Cathedral of Spiritualism, and also President of the Spiritualists' National Union, for which the College was the training ground.

Gordon invited me to the College the following year as a tutor to teach some courses. He said to me, 'We'll never be able to cage you in spiritualism, you'll always need to fly. Your mediumship is so strong because you've had to do it all yourself.'

Some time later, I got into the car and there sitting beside me was a Native American. I asked him his name and he said, 'If it is of importance, my name is Red Cloud.' The name sounded familiar. I was under the impression that that was the name of the guide of a woman I knew but, when I asked her, she said it wasn't. The transcripts of the various sittings I'd done over the last few years were all filed away in a filing cabinet at home. Someone in the group had typed them up, but I had never read them. That day, when I got back I opened a drawer in my bureau and was surprised to find the transcript of a session we'd had at the group. I don't know how it got there. At the bottom of the page I read, 'A new voice spoke, and someone asked who it was, and the answer was; "If it is of importance, my name is Red Cloud."'

A few weeks later I was demonstrating at a church in Stoke-on-Trent. Gordon was in the congregation. Afterwards, he told me that he believed I would work in the manner of Estelle Roberts. Being completely ignorant of the old mediums, I asked some of the people at the church about her. Estelle was a brilliant medium, at her peak between the wars. She would go by name and seat number and give a contact from the spirit world that was very detailed; when she gave a demonstration at the Albert Hall the place would be packed. 'Oh,' I thought, 'that would be nice.' Later, I was telling the librarian of the local Spiritualist Church what had happened and he said;

'Do you know the name of Estelle's guide? It was Red Cloud.'

Unfortunately, Gordon died later that year, a few months before I was due to go to the College. But I went anyway. A few weeks after his death I was demonstrating at Tamworth Church in Staffordshire, and I was giving a contact. I was just describing the woman's house when I saw Gordon and heard his voice as plain as anything.

He started to give me instructions: 'Now go into the lounge, go to the china cabinet, take out a cup, examine it, and describe it.' It was a chipped Royal Doulton cup, which the relative of the contact remembered perfectly. Gordon directed me from the spirit world to send my mind all round the house of the person in spirit. He explained the technique so that I could allow my mind to travel into the mind of those in the spirit world to get all the details about them. For the whole of the demonstration I couldn't believe myself! I would say, 'I want to talk to the woman in the back row, two seats in, I have your father here.' I was then able to give lots of detailed and meaningful information such as full address, the age of passing, and the person's birth-date.

That continued for several demonstrations, and it was great. I felt really sure of myself.

Then, driving to the next one, I stopped at some traffic lights. I actually felt Gordon with me. He said, 'And now you're on your own.' Three years later, I mentioned it to the then President of the Spiritualists' Union, Judith Seamen, and she said that the few mediums who Gordon had taken under his wing were shown how to expand their mediumship and would then be told just that; 'And now you're on your own.'

Gordon taught me to be constantly pushing, not waiting to receive information, but travelling through the consciousness of the person in the spirit world, going further to get things that would give absolute proof to the person listening.

It was my forty-ninth birthday when I first went to the Arthur Findlay College to work as a tutor. It was hard work and long hours, but there were some lovely tutors and great students. It was a joy to work there; to help people to grow within themselves and to see their mediumship blossom was absolutely wonderful.

I made a pledge that if I saw anyone that had the spark of mediumship, I would do everything in my power to help them to develop it. I wouldn't want them to go through what I'd been through. So for the next six years I went to the College for a week or two at a time, often I'd be celebrating my birthday there. And even now, students from four or five years ago still keep in touch.

During this time, I was doing a workshop in Stoke-on-Trent. There was an evening demonstration with another medium. We'd agreed beforehand that we would do two contacts each and then swap over.

Well, after I'd done my two, the other medium did hers but then just went on and on doing more. She carried on for an hour. All the while, I was holding on to a contact. While I was waiting I noticed Hazel, Gordon's sister, in the congregation. She was sitting there smiling at me, looking beautiful.

After a while I started to feel a little uncomfortable. At nearly nine o'clock, when we were due to finish, the chairman said, 'It's your turn, Sue.' She insisted that we carried on. Luckily I managed to hang on to the contact, which was for a woman whose father had just died in the States, and it was very accurate and moving.

After the demonstration Hazel congratulated me on that last contact, and said, 'Did you know that Gordon was standing next to you tonight?' So she'd been smiling all the while at her brother!

'He was standing there all night with his arms folded,' she said. 'When you stood up to do your contacts, he was at your side saying, "Get up and show them what you can do." Did you realise that your demonstration was like Gordon's?'

I said, 'No, I didn't realise that, but I did ask him for a bit of help because my mediumship's been rubbish!' Passionate as ever about mediumship, Gordon is still doing everything he can to help mediums develop. So when I asked, he did help. Maybe if I asked Einstein, he'd come along and give me a bit of brain!

When I'd been going to the College for about eighteen months, I began to get more bookings abroad. I had already started working in Spain some years before. A spiritual awareness group called Cosmos was formed that ran for many years. Cosmos was not confined to the views of Spiritualism so it was a breath of fresh air to me. It's lovely to see that some of those people are still around now that I'm living in Spain. I also started giving workshops and demonstrations in Italy, Switzerland, Australia and Canada, and would sometimes be away for two months at a time.

Once, I was giving sittings at the College during an open week when people would come from all over the country. I was giving a private sitting for a young man who wanted me to contact his father, who was alive but had disappeared some time ago. The young man wanted me to find him, but that wasn't really what I did at all.

I asked the woman doing the bookings to book him in with another medium. Horrified, she said, 'Well, can't you get anything?' I said 'No, I can't, that's not what I do. Will you please see if someone else can help him?'

She finally booked him in with one of the other mediums, but I was fuming. Despite being involved in organising the event, she didn't seem to know the first thing about mediumship!

Later, the demonstration went really smoothly. I transformed the anger that I was feeling to use for the mediumship. Which shows how you can change negative energy into something positive.

Afterwards I was asked to Vancouver Island to work. I enjoyed it tremendously; the students were really great and eager to learn. I ended up going several times.

For five or six years I was travelling all round the world, sometimes with colleagues. It was fun and we had some hilarious times. Which is important, because the work is so intense that you need time to relax and enjoy yourself and be human.

It's interesting that when you're demonstrating abroad you can't give the fine details that you can when at home. Sometimes you get a flash of something but you don't know what it is. The accents are different, the places are unfamiliar, the brand names that people buy and the things they have in their homes are different.

When I had started working in England, I would often get contacts from older people who would talk about things in their homes that I wasn't familiar with, like the old washing machines and mangles and ovens. My daughter lives close to Broadway in the Cotswolds. I used to visit her and go to the local museum in Bourton-on-the-Water and look at some of the old things on display so that when I got a flash of something, I could recognise what I'd seen.

When I was travelling abroad, I found it took me a while to orientate myself. Also, the energy of each country is different so I would have to adjust to the different feel of that country. Before going, I would study a map to try to get an idea of where different places were, so my mind was primed to know where to go. After all, the spirit world doesn't do it all for you; you have to do some work before you can give the same sort of details as you would at home. And it was those extra details that I always liked to give, as they're much more convincing for the people receiving the contact.

CHAPTER SIX

How Mediumship Works:
Questions and Answers

What is the aura?

We are more than a physical body. There is an energy field all around us, which is called our aura. The aura is an electromagnetic field of energy that surrounds every living thing: humans, plants, and animals.

The energy within the aura vibrates at a frequency which is higher than that visible to the naked eye. So we have to use special techniques in order to see it. Kirlian photography was one of the first of these. In 1939, Semyon Kirlian took pictures of the aura from film held in an electrical field. Now, there's also a camera that can take pictures of the auric field; I wonder if it's a hundred per cent accurate, but it does seem to be very popular.

Many years ago, when I came to Spain regularly, a man used to come and see me each time. All he ever wanted to know was what colours I could see in his aura. The thing is, of course, one moment your aura could be quite bright; the next, if you had a pain or a problem, it could be quite different.

That's because our energy field is constantly changing, not just day to day, but minute to minute. Our aura is not fixed, it's in a continuous state of flux as energy moves in and out of our energy field. Likewise the seven chakras (the wheels of energy which constitute the major energy centres of the body) are constantly changing, so that if there is an energy blockage or depletion in one of the chakras one day, it may be gone the next.

If someone suddenly walks up and stands too close to you, it can be quite a shock because, as they step into your auric field, you become uncomfortable and feel that they're invading your personal space.

People with an outgoing personality and lots of self-confidence, for example accomplished actors and actresses, tend to have a very expansive aura. I went once to see Pat Phoenix performing in Birmingham. She was Elsie Tanner in 'Coronation Street', one of the longest-running and most popular soaps in television history. You could actually feel her presence when she walked onto the stage.

Many people, including mediums, can see the aura or sense the energy field. Sometimes, when someone comes into your house, even without seeing him or her, you know that person is upset or unwell. You can sense there's something wrong through their auric field.

When you're working psychically, you're working with the auric field. The aura contains our hopes and desires, our memories, our thoughts and feelings and physical complaints. For a psychic, it's easy to tell someone things about himself purely from looking at, or blending with, his aura. Years ago, my cousin paid ten pounds to go and see a medium and she came back really excited. After hearing some of the things that the medium had said to her, I said, 'You could have asked your mum, she'd have told you that for nothing.'

You hear a lot of strange things about the aura. A medium friend of mine went to a healing circle in her local church in the South of England. She was just sitting peacefully in the circle and was amazed when one of the healers shot out of her chair and ran up behind a woman who'd just come into the church, shouting, 'Stop, stop!' She walked behind the woman, bending over as if picking something up from the floor, like gathering up a bride's train, and said to the woman, 'Your aura's dragging on the floor!' She then walked behind her half-stooped, as if carrying a heavy weight, dragging along the invisible aura.

Another would make as if to lift something heavy, like a monster tea-cosy, off a person before healing, and set it on a chair next to the person, saying, 'I'm just putting your aura to one side in order to give you healing.'

One woman started to gasp, as if catching her breath, and said, 'Oh, I've just trapped my auric field in the door.'

People talk a lot about different levels of the aura. There probably are physical, mental, emotional and spiritual parts of the aura but when I'm sensing it, there's no boundary, there aren't layers where one bit ends and the next begins. People feel bound to put levels on everything; sometimes they try to state facts that aren't facts.

The auric field can depict emotional and physical problems. You can feel any disabilities on a physical level, any things that are wrong with a person. It works for animals too; years ago I went to look at a horse a friend of mine wanted to buy and I could see that it had a problem. From looking at its aura, I could touch right where that problem was, in its flanks, which was later confirmed by the vet.

You can also get a lot of information from the chakras, either by sensing their energy psychically, or by running the hand through the aura, not touching the physical body, but simply feeling the variation in the flow of energy through different chakras.

It seems that there are hundreds of chakras all over the body, but interest focuses on the seven major ones. They're our main energy centres; they connect us to the universe and we draw energy in through them. Some while back, I was showing a friend how to sense into the chakras and she felt that my throat and pelvic areas were completely out; there was little energy circulating there. Shortly after, it turned out that I had hypothyroidism and I also ended up having to have a hysterectomy.

I can always tell if people have difficulty expressing their emotions, simply by looking at their throat chakra. There is often a dark blue band across the throat if they are holding blocked emotions in this area. Often they'll say they suffer from a dry or sore throat, which can be the result of not being able to say what they need to say.

The way I perceive colours is that a highly evolved person has a spiritual presence; his or her aura shimmers, and there is always a silvery colour interlaced with blue. For me, the higher spiritual colours are blue and purple. Very often, when healers are channelling healing energy, I see these colours around them.

As a medium, you shouldn't just use the chakra system or read the aura when you're working, but some mediums do. A lot of information can be gained about a person simply from reading the aura or tuning in to the chakras, but the medium should be able to go straight to the spirit world for information.

What are the different ways of sensing spirit?

There are many different forms of mediumship.

Clairvoyance, or clear seeing, is when a person can actually see those in the spirit world.

All of us can see a person in our mind when they're not there. For example, if you imagine a person you know, you can describe that person and picture him in your mind; you have an image of him although you can't actually see him. Subjectively, you 'see' him. That's how clairvoyance works for many mediums; they see the person in spirit subjectively. Seeing subjectively, it's very fleeting, but you can keep taking your mind back to that image in just the way that you take your mind back to events that happen in everyday life, so that you can describe more and more about that person and strengthen the image in your mind.

Some mediums can see objectively; they see a spirit, in solid form, as clearly as if he had a physical body.

There were about twenty of us at the first mediumship development circle I attended. Afterwards we had a cup of tea. The woman making the tea came in with a tray of teacups and a glass of juice. She said, 'I've made orange juice for the little girl, where's she gone? She was sitting on the couch.' She had seen the little girl in spirit objectively, as if she was really sitting there. This woman was clearly mediumistic but this was the first time that this had happened to her. It was an example of objective seeing in clairvoyance, not of physical mediumship, in which case everyone else in the room would have seen the little girl too.

My mother has seen the spirit world on a few occasions, and she sees them in a solid form. In objective clairvoyance, the spirit appears to have a physical body to the person who is clairvoyant. This is different from materialisation, or physical mediumship, in which the spirit actually appears in solid form and everyone in the room would be able to see it and touch it.

Clairaudience is when a person can hear the spirit world, but again, most clairaudients do not actually hear speech as they would hear it in the physical world. When I hear the spirit world, the thoughts come into my mind without my hearing them, although they're sometimes so clear I can detect an accent as the person speaks.

Other people will hear objectively, as they would hear a physical voice. That has only happened to me twice.

Once, I was in the greenhouse waiting for someone to come for a sitting when I suddenly heard a voice saying; 'Tell her I was late for the wedding.'

When the woman arrived, I told her what I'd heard and she burst into tears. She said, 'Don't tell me any more, I know he's here.' She was convinced simply by that message.

When hearing spirit subjectively, in the mind, one of the problems is that it's not easy to hear everything. You can't stay tuned in for long, so you hear a few words and then you miss some; you hear a few more and miss more, a bit like a person who is hard of hearing. So a message may be missing words, for example you might hear only the 1st, 4th, 6th and 10th words. We don't hear everything and our minds tend to add or interject things to try to make sense of the overall impression.

That's how mediums make mistakes. We can think we know what a person is talking about but we don't and, if we guess at things we haven't heard, or make up the words we've missed, the message can be completely changed like a Chinese whisper. I would often get a quick burst and then have to keep going back into the mind of the person in spirit, rather than fill in the spaces.

On the other hand, of course, the messages are sometimes not what people want to hear. A woman once said to me, 'You told my friend to pack her bags and get out of her marriage.' I said, 'Well, if I say something like that, it's spirit that is talking to me.' It was in fact her friend's grandmother in spirit who had told me, and it was a pity the woman didn't take that advice because her husband later tried to poison her. Why had I not got the bit about the attempted poisoning? Perhaps I just missed it, or maybe it would have been too difficult for the woman to hear at that time. I don't know.

Clairsentience to me is a wonderful form of mediumship, though perhaps I just say that because it's my strongest. Working with clairsentience, as with all forms of mediumship, the medium's mind has to travel into the mind of the person in spirit. Although to the observer you look normal, you can actually feel the spirit world. It's as though you're slipping into the auric field of the person in spirit, like putting on a glove. You can describe that person, their physical characteristics, their mannerisms and quirky little habits. A training medium once told a student that clairsentience was the lowest form of mediumship. I found this very sad because all mediumship is wonderful, and she could have done with a bit herself.

Once, at Smethwick Church in the West Midlands, a spirit wanted me to go to his daughter in the congregation and put something in her hand. Normally we weren't supposed to leave the platform, but I was always one to break the rules so I said to the chairman I was going to go down. The chairman said, 'Oh, Sue, you do what you like.' Walking down the stairs there were three little steps and, without thinking, my leg shot out in front of me. I automatically bent over and hit it back from the straight to the bent position. At that, the woman shouted out, 'Oh my God, it's my dad, that's exactly what he used to do. He had a wooden leg and used to have to bang it with his hand when it got stuck.'

It would be nice to think that once we pass away our physical ailments are gone straight away. Of course, for many people there is a quick realisation that they are whole again. Some people, however, take a time to adjust to their new state of being.

Many years ago a neighbour, Sandra, came to see me and we later became friends. Her mother had passed away some little time before. Although she lived quite close to me and I had given her mother healing in the past, I knew very little of the last year or so of her mother's life because of my busy schedule.

After the communication had been established, I kept feeling as if I was going to fall over. I wasn't dizzy or anything, I just felt as if I couldn't stand up. When I told Sandra she said that her mother had had both her legs amputated before she left this life. So, although she was obviously mentally and emotionally quite at home in her new life, she had not yet realised that the loss of her legs was merely a memory carried over from this life.

Some time later, Sandra came to see me again. Her mother was anxious to speak to her and it was a joy to help in the communication. After a while I felt compelled to stand up and simply say, 'Look at me, and I can dance again too.'

It may be very hard to believe but I had no idea what that was all about. At that time I was seeing hundreds of people every year and couldn't remember anything that had been said at any particular reading. Occasionally something unusual would happen and I would be able to recall it, but for the vast majority of readings I honestly had no recollection at all. So I had forgotten what had happened at the first sitting.

Sandra reminded me that the last time I had talked to her mother, her mother still felt that she could not walk. After just passing into the spirit world she had, through the power of her mind, recreated her inability to walk, which, although obviously merely a mental state, was still very real to her. Now, just a few months later, she had had the realisation that her body was whole again. Not only could she walk again but she could dance too, something that she'd loved doing when she was younger.

So I would pick up the physical characteristics or personality traits of the person in spirit. If it was a very houseproud woman, I'd be cleaning bits and pieces and putting them straight while speaking to her relative, without even realising I was doing it.

At the College I was doing a trance demonstration. There were several mediums working that night. I was describing the grandmother of one of my friends, who was also a medium. When my friend came to sit beside me, I held her hand. It had a waxy feeling. She said later that it felt exactly like her gran's hand. I opened her hand and closed it again as if to put something in it, and she said, 'That's what my gran used to do when she gave me a sixpence pocket money.'

In addition, there's also just **clairknowing**, which is when we just simply know something. All the three clairs, clairvoyance, clairaudience and clairsentience are probably involved in some way. I don't know how it works, but it does.

Trance mediumship. All mediums work in an altered state of consciousness, but with trance mediums it's a deeper state of altered consciousness. The purpose of trance is that a medium can go into trance and channel information that would not necessarily be known to them or to people around them; they can go way back into the past or into the future, as with precognition. The medium's conscious mind is bypassed. The medium is just a channel through which the mind in the spirit world speaks.

I believe that when in a trance state the medium should be able to bring wisdom from the spirit world. But I know one trance medium who would always answer any questions with another question, therefore never really giving any answers. At their very best, trance mediums speak directly to higher evolved spirits, bringing wonderful philosophy from the spirit world without intermediaries. It has also been known for trance mediums to speak in other languages.

However, there's a lot of pseudo-trance about. I'm always surprised when mediums purporting to work in trance are back to their normal selves within a minute of coming out of trance. For me, it's a bit like after an anaesthetic, it takes some time to come round.

In a trance the words just come; you've got no control over them; you say them but you're not aware of what you're saying. A deep trance medium would not even hear the words he was saying, he would appear to be fast asleep; you can pinch him and there's no response.

One story was told to me by a well-known medium. He went to a trance circle given by a development group in a Spiritualist Church in the North of England. When he got there, the chairs were set out and everything was prepared. Ten people were sitting in the circle and, after a while, one man started breathing really quickly. The medium was quite alarmed and said, 'This man's hyperventilating, we must do something.' The President of the Church said, 'That's ok, leave him, this is normal for him.' After a short while the man stood bolt upright with his hands on his hips, then he fell flat on his face with his palms facing upwards and outwards and just lay there. The medium was astounded. He looked at the President who said, 'Oh, no, that's alright, he's been entranced by a kipper.'

Is it any wonder people don't want to go to development groups!

Transfiguration is quite rare these days. The most well-known transfiguration medium was Ena Twigg. When she was in a trance, the face of the person in spirit with whom she was talking would appear in front of her face, like a mask, so that you could actually see that person.

In order to do this, the medium must have physical mediumship. Years ago, in Spain, it happened to a student of mine. It was hot, broad daylight, and we were doing a workshop in a hotel.

Suddenly, San Lo was with me and I found myself saying, 'Everybody come and sit together, bring your chairs and sit here.' I asked one woman to sit on a chair in the middle of the group, in front of everyone. Her name was Jane and she was from the Philippines. I said, 'Close your eyes, relax and think nice thoughts, think of nice places.'

Suddenly a face appeared in front of Jane's. Almost instantly everyone in the room saw faces coming in front of hers. One of the students in the group, Tanya, was slightly deaf. She didn't hear what I was saying but she said later it hit her in the stomach, like a punch in her solar plexus, when she saw the first face.

The spirit world was using energy from all the people in the room, but Tanya could feel it more than some of the others as she had so much energy. And she could see the faces appearing without hearing what was going on.

It was always said that transfiguration had to take place in a darkened room with everyone squinting to see if they could see anything, but obviously a lot of these Victorian ideas no longer hold.

Transfiguration and trance can be enhanced by the energy of the house we're sitting in, or the environment and even the country, which is why a medium will often have one room set aside in their house to use for their mediumship. The vibration is very heavy, and it used to make me feel quite ill when people were sitting for me to go into a trance.

Materialisation, or physical mediumship, requires a physical medium who is able to produce a spirit in solid form from a substance called ectoplasm. Every person in the room will be able to see the spirit, who will usually walk over to their loved one, talk to him and touch him. Materialised spirits feel human; they are warm and solid to the touch.

There are many people who have had such experiences. However, physical mediumship does seem to be on the wane at present, perhaps partially because of all the electrical interference around. There are very few materialisation mediums as it takes a long time to develop that ability, and people don't have the time or dedication to do it much now. It must be wonderful to see, but it clearly hasn't made as much impact as the spirit world might have hoped.

When I have enquired of my helpers from the spirit world, they have told me that the impact of physical mediumship could not be the same in the fast moving 21st century. In recent times physical mediumship has made little difference to the world, unlike two thousand years ago when Christ was seen resurrected from the grave and was able to make Himself manifest in solid form through the strength of His disciples' mediumship.

My spirit guides described Jesus and His disciples as the greatest mediums man has ever known.

Direct voice mediumship. The medium must be a physical medium in order for this phenomenon to occur. A trumpet is used, a cone-shaped piece of metal about eighteen inches long. The cone flies around the room and stops in front of someone who then hears his loved one's voice talking directly to him. The best-known direct voice medium was Leslie Flint.

Psychic art is another example of how mediumship can be used.

I remember years ago a psychic artist came to the church. Her first drawing was of a face completely wrapped in bandages with two holes for the eyes, so no one could recognise who it was. She then drew a face and said, 'There's a little boat up its nose, this person must have liked boats.' She was never booked at that church again!

Recently, the world's foremost psychic artist was Coral Polge; she had the ability to draw the faces of people in the spirit world, sometimes with such accuracy that it was just like a photograph. Although she was mediumistic, she would always work with a medium. She would establish the contact, tune in and start drawing the face. When she began saying things about the contact, the medium would tune in too, and give the communication while she carried on drawing.

She was an absolute joy to work with. The first demonstration I ever did at the College was with Coral. The communication was going beautifully while Coral was drawing the woman's face. Then the woman said, 'She hasn't got my earrings on there.' I was in two minds whether I'd dare tell Coral, but I did and she took it in good spirit.

Su Wood, from Stourbridge in the West Midlands, is a superb psychic artist. Although she had no artistic training and claimed she couldn't even draw a straight line she suddenly found herself drawing spirit faces! Even when she'd just started, the likenesses she could produce of people in the spirit world were quite astounding. Another very good psychic artist, also from the Midlands, is Gerald

Townsend-Howes who works with his wife Sue, an excellent medium in her own right. So psychic art seems to be an area of mediumship that's growing at the moment.

Ouija boards and table-tilting; some people still use these to contact spirit, but I don't know why. I can't see the validity of them in this day and age. But in the past they were very popular.

A ouija board has the letters of the alphabet all round it, with a pointer that moves to each letter. We used to make our own. When I was about seventeen I worked in the secretarial department of the Co-op in Birmingham with about six other girls all of a similar age, and it became our daily lunch-time activity when we weren't shopping for clothes. We'd use it to find out who would be our next boyfriend; according to the ouija board, whoever we were going out with at the time was always our husband-to-be. Talk about wishful thinking!

There was an elderly lady called Mrs Christmas, who once found us doing it. She warned us off, saying, 'You don't know what forces you're playing with.'

One lunchtime I went into the room where we ate and played our ouija game. There was no one about. Suddenly I heard a knocking, then a silence, and then another three knocks. I was terrified and started saying, 'Hello, is there anybody there?' Just at that moment, Mrs Christmas came in. She could see how frightened I was and I told her what I'd heard. She said, 'Well, I have warned you!' and walked out. As I turned to watch her go, I caught a glimpse of my friend Mo sitting under the very large table that we used. The other girls had been hiding in the cupboards. When they came out, Mo was laughing so much at my terror that she wet herself!

I have seen ouija boards used by mediums, but I never felt that the information was terribly convincing and could never understand why they bothered with a clumsy ouija board if they could contact spirit using their mind. The sale of boards stopped some years ago because they were felt to be dangerous; it had been reported that the tables had at times become out of control and people had even been thrown against the wall. The problem is that many people without mediumistic abilities do it just as a game and, without a medium there to see what is really going on, people could be attracting all sorts of angry, mischievous spirits. Or it could have been their own psychic energy or emotions making the pointer or the glass or the table move.

In table-tilting, mediums used to put their hands on a table and it would move around the room, stop in front of somebody, and then people would ask questions. They had to wait for each name or word to be spelled out; the leg of the table would tap on the floor a number of times for each letter of the alphabet. It was all very laborious.

Table-tilting was a favourite of one particular course organizer at the College, so we usually had to demonstrate it during the week's course.

One week, I'd given a sitting to a man; his seven-year-old son had communicated and it had been very moving and emotional. The following day, we gave a demonstration of table-tilting. It was a large room and there were about sixty people sitting in a circle. Suddenly the table started moving so fast our hands couldn't even touch it. It was going all over the place as if in excitement. One of the mediums chided it, whereupon it almost jumped into the lap of the man to whom I'd given the sitting the previous day. I recognised the energy of his seven-year-old son.

In the archives of the College of Psychic Studies at Stansted Hall, a mechanical ouija board was found, a large metal contraption, like a metal table standing on its own legs. It was quite big, about two feet in diameter, and on the top were numbers and letters. Underneath, there was a lever and a pendulum hanging down with a weight on the end. The hope was that the board would move on its own.

I once saw it being used. There were six mediums and one guy was supposed to be in trance, but all the while he was making sexual remarks to one of the women. Well, after an hour nothing had happened and some of us were fed up and disgusted. Then I saw the guy kick the lever underneath and suddenly the pointer started to move. Three of us saw him do it. The others in the group, though, thought that spirits had arrived to order!

Apports are material objects that suddenly appear without any explanation, and are said to be produced by spirit. Many people report having received all sorts of apports. Although there are many genuine instances, this is a form of mediumship that is particularly open to abuse as the meetings are often conducted in total darkness.

One of the stories I like best occurred at the College. A visiting medium was sitting as if in trance, waiting for apports. The heavy curtains were drawn and it was very dark. Suddenly a ball fell onto the chandelier, which made everyone suspicious. Why would spirit throw a ball onto a chandelier? But someone had seen the medium throw it and he was quickly marched off the premises. The College would never knowingly tolerate fraudulent mediumship and the man was banned from the College.

Sadly, people make up all sorts of things that give true mediumship a bad name. Some years before, another medium would produce roses, until it was discovered he used to hide a bunch of roses in a large tape-recorder and then get them out in the dark. He was later exposed in the *Psychic News*.

I once saw a medium in London who was said to work with apports. He was an Indian Swami. Everyone was really impressed with him. He was sitting in the lotus position on a bench surrounded by little boxes. I had to sit in front of him on the floor and he talked to me about different spiritual levels. He said that I was at level three. I still don't know what that meant. I must just be stuck there! He then told me to close my eyes, but I peeped and heard a rustling of tissue paper. When he said I could open my eyes, he showed me his empty hand, palm upwards, turned it over, closed his fist, opened his hand again and there was a nut, which he solemnly gave to me. Perhaps it was symbolic!

There was a place somewhere in the South-East of England that was set up to investigate physical mediumship. A man I know went to see what they were doing. He managed to get in and came back very impressed. He said that a materialised hand was going round in front of everyone.

I said, 'Did you see it?'

He said, 'No, it was too dark.'

Near Telford, in Shropshire, a development group met regularly for years in their old church, probably in the dark. They could hear a little tapping noise all the time and used to say, 'God bless you, friends.' This went on for years until one day the floor fell in. It had death-watch beetles and the whole floor collapsed. Presumably they picked up their brains on the way out. At least they could see the funny side later and had a laugh about it.

What makes a good medium?

In my opinion, a good medium is an honest person who has a real desire to work on behalf of the spirit world and not for his or her own ego. S/he needs to have integrity and compassion for those on earth as well as those in spirit. I would say that to be a good medium you have to have a lot of self-discipline. You also have to be able to close off to the spirit world when you're not working.

Different mediums will appeal to different people, but a good medium is one who will keep working on himself, continuing to question and trying to stretch his mediumship to work in honesty and truth.

As with everything, there are good 'uns and there are bad 'uns. Anyone can set up as a medium. The Fraudulent Mediums Act has never been used as far as I know, but unfortunately there are a lot of frauds about who have no qualms about taking advantage of vulnerable people. So to a large extent it's trial and error to find what you consider to be a good medium. There are clearly people who suffer at the hands of frauds, not least the genuine mediums who get tarred with the same brush.

Many mediums are working quietly in their own homes. Plenty of people have found comfort and joy from their local medium. I wouldn't advise a person to go to a medium who advertises. A good medium doesn't need to. Their reputation travels by word of mouth.

I believe that there should be some standard of practice. The trouble is, I can't see how it would work: there are mediums, like myself, who have passed exams in the SNU to prove their mediumship, but qualifications do not necessarily ensure good mediumship.

A good medium is one who can give detailed and accurate information about the spirit world. If you say, 'I have an elderly lady here, she's short with grey hair, around sixty,' and you ask people in the audience to stand up if they think they recognise her, then half the audience might rise from their seats, thinking it could be their long-lost grandmother. If, after a few more minutes of description, there are eight people still standing then you're not being specific enough.

General information that could apply to anyone is no good; you have to be specific and tune into those intimate details and characteristics that will leave the person in the audience in no doubt that the spirit wanting to communicate is actually their grandmother.

People want so much for their loved one to be there. They can be so vulnerable and needy at this time, particularly if the death is recent, that they might be satisfied with information that really doesn't do justice to the spirit world.

Sometimes the information given by a medium is so vague and imprecise as to be ridiculous.

I once heard a medium say to a young man, 'I've got your mother in the spirit world.'

'No,' the man said, 'my mum's still here.'

'It's your grandmother, then.'

'No, she's alive and well.'

'It's your sister, then.'

'I haven't got one.'

'Your auntie?'

'No,' said the man.

In desperation, the medium said, 'It must be your uncle, and he's telling me that you're bouncing balls off a bat all the time. He's saying you'll know what he means.'

The young man got up and walked out. I don't blame him.

Who do you consider were the great mediums?

There have been many outstanding mediums over the years.

Helen Duncan was an outstanding physical medium who spent her life giving proof of life after death. Often those who had died would appear in solid, physical form. During the Second World War, she was receiving messages from dead soldiers and sailors including information such as the names of the ships, where they had gone down, and how many lives had been lost. Seen as a threat to the establishment, she was charged in 1944 under the Witchcraft Act and imprisoned for nine months. The trial was given much publicity. In 1956, the police raided a séance, grabbed Helen while she was in the middle of materialisation and took many photographs. She became ill as a result of this and two months later she was dead.

Albert Best was an old man when I met him, a small Irishman who had lived in Glasgow most of his life. He was appearing at my local Spiritualist Church in Sutton Coldfield. At the last moment, the chairperson was taken ill and I was called to stand in as chair. I was terrified as I'd never done that, although I had demonstrated mediumship publicly before.

Albert was walking calmly up and down outside the church, smoking his beloved Park Drive cigarettes, while the church filled to capacity. People were even standing in the hallway. When we walked on to the platform the atmosphere was electric. To watch him was pure joy. At one point he was speaking to an elderly man sitting in the back row. Albert was a little deaf so he couldn't hear the man's responses but carried on with his message anyway. The man had been a drummer who often played with the then famous Issy Bonn band. Albert mentioned every musician by name and the instrument they'd played, and everyone laughed when he told the man that he'd once made a right balls-up of his introduction. 'Yes,' the man agreed, delighted, 'Issy never let me forget that.'

Albert's wife and two children had been killed when their tenement was bombed during the Second World War. He used to travel all round the world demonstrating mediumship. On a trip to Africa he met a witch doctor, obviously a physical medium, who was able to make his wife and children materialise.

'They appeared in solid form and I danced with them in the middle of Africa,' he said, showing me a tattered photo of his family that he always carried in his breast pocket.

Albert reminded me of my dad. He was honest and straightforward and modest. In those days, twenty years ago, it was two pounds to go in to the demonstration and, because I was the Chairperson that day, I said Albert should be paid thirty pounds. His face lit up, as the Church would have been happy to give him a fiver.

Quiet and unassuming, he always respected confidentiality. It was well known that he was a medium for the Queen Mother and the Gandhi family. Yet he told me that he never felt comfortable in grand places. In fact, during his visits to the Gandhi family he even insisted on washing his underpants himself!

He had worked as a postman for most of his life. So he would give not only the first name and surname of the contact in the spirit world, but also their full address and post-code. Such accurate detail left even cynics and non-believers truly amazed.

He was a medium in the finest sense.

Alex Harris was a well-known and much respected materialisation medium. I never met him, but a friend of mine, Norma, had seen him many years ago when she was a young girl.

Norma is an accomplished artist and writer and has been involved in Spiritualism since childhood. I had known her for some years. She lost her husband when she was in her sixties. She told me that she knew he was fine and alive and she needn't cry for his passing, although people kept telling her that she should. I asked her why she was so sure; even as a working medium I sometimes still had my doubts.

She told me that when she was young she lived in Barry, South Wales, and her father was the Treasurer of the South Wales Council of the Spiritualists' National Union. When she was fifteen, he saved up ten shillings so that he could take her and her mother and brother to see Alex Harris.

Mediumship was illegal in those days so they had gone one by one to the small miner's cottage where Alex was holding a séance. They were each shown into a small bedroom where a group of eight people eventually gathered.

Everyone was sitting in the narrow, darkened room. Everything was quiet. Suddenly a Native American appeared, from what was actually ectoplasm but appeared to be mist. The Indian welcomed them all to the evening and pointed out where Alex was sitting in a deep trance state in the corner behind him, to all intents fast asleep.

The Native American walked round the circle and accidentally trod on Norma's toes. She let out a yell because he was quite heavy. He apologised and asked her if she would like to touch his feathers. She wanted to, of course, and she told me that he put his arms around her waist and lifted her high in the air to touch his headdress, the colours and hues of which she'd never seen on this earth.

He said that he knew that some people would think he was fake so he would ask two figures from the spirit world to draw close, in order to prove that there was no trickery. As he said this, two figures grew from within the mist, both in cloaks, which they opened to reveal a male and a female form. Well, this was just the beginning. Over the next hour many more appeared in the room, in solid form, to talk to their loved ones. After a short while Norma heard her voice being called and the shape of a friend of hers started to build in the room. This friend had died when she was ten or eleven.

'Did you recognise her?' I asked.

'Of course I did. I held her hand and felt her heartbeat, and we spoke for ten minutes. She was so excited talking about all our friends at school. Then when she was going, it was just like wax melting in my hand. And the mist went down into the ground as she disappeared.'

Roy was a brilliant untrained and natural medium whom I first met thirty years ago; unfortunately I don't remember his surname. He was a very popular medium and his messages were very accurate. A small, gentle, balding man, he worked on the floor of one of the many car-producing factories that were around the Midlands at that time.

He used to go into a trance and his breathing would change. It always reminded me of the wind blowing the leaves in autumn. He would then do a ritual dance, his arms swinging around and his feet moving at such a rate they became just a blur; at times it was almost as if he was hovering above the ground. Why he did that is still a mystery to me!

After a short while, when it looked as if he was about to expire, he would clap his hands together three times, clap them on his legs three times, and proclaim in a loud voice, 'Good evening, it is so good to be with you once again!' He would then stand with his hands clasped around his mouth and blow repeatedly. We nicknamed him The Glassblower.

After this, he would walk round the circle of anxious sitters, shaking their hands with such vigour that those who were well versed in his ways would slip off their rings to avoid their fingers being crushed.

Then he was ready to begin. In this altered state, Roy was clairsentient. He would completely take on the persona of the person in spirit. I have seen him glide gracefully around the room singing the favourite tune of someone on the other side. He would then stop in front of someone in the circle, who would know precisely who the dancer was. He would use different intonations of speech and phrasing. He would walk as if drunk and then almost fall into the lap of the exact person who would know the drunken man who had just called to say he loved them!

One night he stood in front of my mum and sang a song in a certain way, using words that only my dad would use. My beloved dad was there; I knew it without a doubt, not just by the words but also because I could sense him.

Roy brought love, joy and plenty of laughter from the spirit world. He brightened so many people's lives, reassuring them that they had not lost their loved ones, giving them the knowledge that they would one day be reunited.

But his mediumship was so good and he was so popular that the man and wife team who ran the circle were completely overcast as mediums when Roy was around. He was gradually eased out of the circle by a series of ridiculous disagreements and accusations. Which was a great pity.

Two or three years later, Alan Wardell, now one of my oldest friends, joined the group. He knew nothing about Roy, but within a few months he started doing exactly the same dance, the same sequence of clapping and blowing, with the same opening words, 'Good evening, it is so good to be with you again!' The delivery of the messages was exactly the same.

Alan was another excellent natural medium. It was obvious that the Native American who had worked through Roy was now working through Alan although Roy was still alive. Some people at the group used to insist that their spirit guide would only work through them, but this shows clearly that it's not necessarily so.

Glyn Edwards, from Liverpool (not to be mistaken for the actor who played Dave, the barman in 'Minder'), is a brilliant medium. He is always elegantly dressed and has a beautiful speaking voice. In fact he is known as the Golden Voice of Spiritualism. He is one of the best demonstrating mediums in the UK at the moment. Some of the information he gives from the platform is astounding, and the places are usually full to capacity whenever he works. If anyone has the chance to go and see him, I would highly recommend it.

Gordon Smith also has an excellent reputation as a medium. Although I have never met him, I saw him on television recently. I was impressed by the accuracy of his mediumship and by his down to earth manner and no-nonsense approach.

What happens in a private sitting?

A private sitting is an opportunity for a person to communicate with someone in the spirit world. As I said before, I would often ask the person to send out thoughts to their loved one in the spirit world for a few days prior to coming for their sitting.

I always used to record the session and give people the tape when they came for a private sitting, as often so much information was given that it couldn't all be assimilated at once. There were times when the tape-recorder was switched on and going round but at the end the tape would be blank. Sometimes it just wouldn't work, I don't know why. There was a time in Italy when people would bring several tape-recorders in, as various sounds had been reported on the tape in the background.

The spirit world does seem to be able to affect electronic equipment in some way. I'm reminded of the time when a woman had just been talking to her husband in the sitting. As she went to go out the door, the radio came on of its own accord. When she heard the song, she said in amazement, 'That's our tune!'

Spirit can also make lights flicker and computers go on or off. Sometimes a spirit would say, 'You know that bedside light that's always flickering, that's me trying to let you know I'm here.' Though others will say, 'Don't blame that faulty light on me, it's not me doing it!' Just as in life here, everyone's different.

Val was a neighbour of mine who I once did a counselling course with. She was strikingly good-looking, tall, and used to be a model. She was also a real character whom you couldn't help but like.

She had been diagnosed with a brain tumour, so I took her with another friend of mine, Ann, to see Steve Turoff in Chelmsford, Essex. He is a well-known psychic surgeon. One of the Sunday papers had published an article on him a while before, including a photo of him putting a pair of scissors up the nose of a fully conscious patient! When we walked in and Ann saw the photograph, she was so scared she almost ran out of the room. I had to hold on to her and sit her down in the chair.

We were all nervous and giggly as we went in. I had an operation with him, which was successful. Unfortunately Val's wasn't. She died very young. She had a tremendous fighting spirit though.

Some time later, a young lady came for a sitting. I didn't know her although she was local. The session was going along as usual when suddenly I was very aware of the presence of Val. I was somewhat taken aback. I apologised to the woman and told her that a friend of mine who lived more or less opposite had recently died with a brain tumour.

It turned out that the woman was a close friend of Val's and had nursed her during the last months of her illness. They were overjoyed to see each other and the three of us talked at length. Val was concerned for her young son who was living with her ex-husband. Her friend said that she saw both of them regularly and they were fine. This put Val's mind at rest.

There are occasionally times when a contact is made and a message given, yet the person receiving it doesn't want to accept it. Some years ago a young woman came to see me, and her mother communicated from the spirit world. The mother was terribly upset and kept saying to her daughter, 'I'm so sorry for what happened.'

When I gave this message to the woman, she wouldn't listen and started to project all her anger onto me.

I said, 'I'm just saying what your mother is telling me.'

'It's too late now,' she said.

If that's how she felt, I wondered why she had come. I don't know what she was expecting to hear but, whatever it was, I wasn't able to fulfil her needs. She didn't want to work on her own anger and however much her mother apologised, she just wouldn't accept it.

There were a few times when I was giving a private sitting that I couldn't get anything at all. If I didn't sense the spirit within the first ten minutes, I'd say, 'Sorry, there's nothing there, it's not working. Come back another time and we'll try again.' I've heard all sorts of excuses from mediums as to why their mediumship wouldn't work on a particular day, but all I would say is that the person you're working with has to be really open and willing to give their own energy to aid the process.

Thank goodness most of my sittings didn't come through the Spiritualist Church. They used to tell people going for a sitting not to say a word. Which of course just made it more difficult. I couldn't see the point of that. And why should the person not say what s/he wants to say? Imagine someone standing in front of you, speaking to you, and you not answering a word! Why would you want to put someone in spirit through that?

Generally speaking, though, my sittings went very well. Some lovely people came to see me, many of whom kept in touch afterwards, even sending flowers and cards when I was poorly. It was nice to know that I'd gained their respect.

Some people have said that a sitting has completely changed their life. Doreen, who later became a friend, came to me for a sitting and spoke to her mother. Doreen had been brought up as a Catholic and had never believed in the spirit world but, after that experience, she started going to awareness classes and looking into Spiritualism. It wasn't that there had been any particular unresolved issues with her mother, it was just that the sheer joy of realising that she was still there changed her view of life and death.

I certainly don't want to have bitterness or hatred or jealousy when I go. For me, mediumship has made me much more aware of myself; it has compelled me to take responsibility for who and what I am.

Receiving proof of life after death does change the way you think. It makes you look at yourself in a different way; you start to question where you come from, what you're doing, and your reactions to events and other people. It can give people the urge to make the most of this life, to try to change things while they're here. And it helps them to cope with some of the difficulties of this life.

Mediums and healers are no more special than anyone else. Everybody on earth is special; sometimes that's difficult to believe or to act on, but it is a fact. It's just that some people are a little more lost than others. Happily, there are increasing numbers of people on earth now who are conscious of their spiritual journey, and being given personal insight into the spirit world helps to affirm their beliefs and to encourage them on their path.

But there are others who are just purely concerned with themselves, with having a bigger house, designer clothes, luxury holidays, and the rest of it. That is all very nice, but what about the other journey that is waiting to be explored? Material things cannot give us the sort of contentment that we get from knowing God, whether that's the part of God that is within us, or the great eternal energy that we call God. Once we've found that, we have all the riches in the world.

What happens in a demonstration?

Every medium will approach a demonstration in his or her own individual way. I found that I would start preparing by sending out my thoughts to the spirit world and to my helper some hours before. However, when a demonstration was part of a workshop, I didn't always have the luxury of that time.

To demonstrate in public requires a skill that only experience can bring, and unfortunately many mediums who worked very well in small groups were pushed onto the platform too early – maybe to fill a gap when the guest mediums didn't show up – and the whole experience would be so terrifying to them that they never wanted to do it again.

The Spiritualist Church always had a lot of rules about how a medium should do a demonstration. They were trained to work with the person first and then go to the spirit world, but I hadn't had any training so I would go straight to the spirit world because that's how it came to me. I would never know which person in the audience I was going to. My mind would go to the spirit world. I would describe that person in spirit, often in great detail, and then ask if anyone knew this person and could accept the contact.

I used to come across a great deal of prejudice about the way I worked. One evening I did a demonstration at Stourbridge Church in the West Midlands. It went particularly well and I was back there again the next Monday afternoon. The church was packed. I was told that was because the news of the Sunday night demonstration had got around. Again it was a good demonstration, giving absolute evidence of life after death. But afterwards the Treasurer came into the side room, stood there sternly and said to me, 'I like it when a medium knows who the contact is for.' My way of working had always been to establish the link with a contact first, and then ask the audience if anyone recognised that person in spirit.

So my reply to him was, 'When I'm told to by spirit, I'll do it like that, but in the meantime I work my way.'

I had already gained a reputation as a good platform medium. I was confident. But imagine how terrifying that comment would be to someone just starting out. In fact, quite a few inexperienced mediums were afraid to go to certain churches because of the critical attitude of some of the committee members.

When Gordon Higginson taught at the College, he suggested that every contact should take six minutes. How can you put a time on a contact from the spirit world? In a demonstration lasting an hour and a half, I would rather give eight meaningful, in-depth contacts, rather than sixteen hurried or superficial ones.

I often used to work with two or three other mediums, particularly when raising money for charity. This was easier as we could share the time between us. If they were generous they would have positive thoughts in their minds when another medium was working.

There was a rule, when demonstrating in Spiritualist Churches, that the medium never left the platform. Always the rebel, I would often leave the platform, which didn't go down very well, but of course it didn't detract one jot from the quality of the mediumship. The rule was also that the mediums should dress soberly, the men in suits, even in summer, and the women in dark colours with long sleeves. Trousers for women were frowned upon, but I never wore anything else, and certainly would not wear clothes that I was not comfortable in. I fought long and hard, and eventually the rules were changed. Women mediums are now allowed to wear trousers on platform.

There was an unstated rule that we should be serious throughout the demonstration, no jokes or laughter allowed. Which to be honest could make the whole business a little dull. Especially as the joy of spirit is such a wonder to experience that I would always like to share it. I often found that when people were moved and uplifted by their own personal contacts with the spirit world, the whole audience would feel joyful and happy, and laughter just came naturally.

I believe that everyone has to find his or her own best way of working. Rules that say, 'This is how mediumship must work' not only limit the potential of the individual medium, because it's simply not the right way for him to work, but they also limit the spirit world and how those in spirit are able to work with the medium.

Mediumship to me is a joyous experience. It's such a wonderful feeling when a demonstration has gone well, there are simply no words to describe it. Over the years many people attending my demonstrations have told me that they felt that joy, and were uplifted by the spirit world, although obviously not all of them had personally had a contact with their loved ones.

I didn't always get to speak to people after a demonstration, so I wouldn't really know what it had set in motion for them. For many people, receiving proof of life after death is just the beginning of a possibly far-reaching process. As I'd often be moving on and going somewhere else, especially when I was working abroad, I'd never see those people again. I can only hope that the joy of spirit has stayed with them and brought positive changes in their lives. I know it has for me.

When I was working, I always had the sense of optimism and joy and humour that comes from being in contact with spirit. Now that I've retired, I miss that. So maybe I'll have to reconsider and start working again.

What factors affect a medium's sensitivity?

Our mediumship is not consistent. Firstly, to put it simply, we're human. Secondly, certain outside influences will affect it. Thirdly, our own beings play such an important part in the interactive process between medium and spirit.

Years back, when they electrified the railway in front of Sutton Coldfield Church, Professor Eric Hills, who invented the post code for the UK, came to the church to give a talk and demonstration on dowsing. He predicted that mediums would find it more difficult to work because of the electrical fields induced around those power lines. It's interesting that physical mediumship, which requires an enormous amount of energy, is much more rare these days, possibly because there are so many things that interfere with the energy coming through to the medium's mind – satellites, for instance, radio masts, mobile phones.

I find particularly that electrical fields and computers interfere with my energy and mediumship. Once, Dave and I were driving along under a long row of high-tension electricity lines. I shut my eyes and could tell him each time there was a cable overhead because I could feel the difference as we drove under each of the lines. I often feel ill when sitting in front of a computer.

Some mediums are sensitive to loud music, bright lights, or crowded rooms. I used to find that the frequency of the air conditioning and even the tumble dryer would make me feel quite ill and faint.

Mediumship can also be affected by the climate and weather conditions. I was working by the Malvern Hills in Worcestershire, getting some contacts and trying to build up others. All evening it was hard work. On my way home there was a thunderstorm.

Gordon Higginson said that weather could affect mediumship, in which case you would have to rely on your psychic ability. Another medium used to say her mediumship was at its best when the moon was full.

So, mediumship can be affected by various outside influences, such as a negative atmosphere, electrical energy, or bad weather, and also by internal factors, such as the medium's own cycle or mood.

Stress and emotional problems can completely shut down your mediumship skills. After all, to be clairsentient, you have to be completely open. I remember a time when I was disillusioned with many of the people I'd worked with. I found I couldn't feel any spirit at all. It was heart-breaking.

What are the dangers of mediumship?

Mediums are right-brained, so they're not always very rational and their minds tend to flit around a lot. But it's surprising how many seem to lose their common sense altogether once they get involved with the spirit world.

Two members of the church at Sutton Coldfield were both mediumistic. Whenever there was a noise in the house or the wind blew down the chimney, they would say, 'God bless you, friend,' because they'd think it must be a spirit trying to contact them. Once they were sitting at home having a cup of tea after finishing their shift at the factory when, through the French windows, they saw a mist drifting across the bottom of the garden. 'God bless you, come closer, friend,' they said again, and walked the whole length of the garden talking to the mist, to encourage the spirit they thought was there. A few minutes later, when great billows of smoke were blowing past, they finally realised that someone was having a bonfire a few gardens down!

Another thing people used to say was that if you were giving a sitting, and had a spirit contact there, you would break the link if you crossed your arms, or if someone walked between you and the person receiving the message during a demonstration.

Clearly, such silliness and superstition don't do mediums or mediumship any favours at all!

Another problem arises when mediums don't learn to close off from the spirit world. If they spend too much time in contact with spirit and not enough time doing physical, mundane things to ground themselves, they end up going around with their heads in the clouds, spaced out and completely ungrounded. And that's not healthy.

If you're not consciously aware that you're sensing things and you don't close down to it then, as you go about your daily life, you can be picking up other people's emotions, the atmosphere of a place, arguments or negative energy and all sorts of things without even realising it. Various people and situations can make you feel upset and even ill.

Mediums have to be sensitive in order to attune to frequencies that other people are not aware of, but the downside of this is that we're often too sensitive and tend to overreact to everyday events. Mediums with any depth to their mediumship can be quite temperamental, volatile and quick to take offence. Or we can suffer from mood swings or become depressed. As we're bringing the energy through the root chakra a lot of the time, we can also become very sexual and form impulsive attractions to people, which can cause problems in our relationships.

Mediumship is interactive, not passive. Mediums often have poor physical health as they are using such a tremendous amount of energy all the time. They are also using the adrenal system every time they're working. Diabetes and hypothyroidism are particularly common in mediums. The immune system can also be affected; all sorts of illnesses may occur, especially when working very regularly.

One of my husband's concerns was always my health, as he'd observed how many mediums became ill. Now, since retiring, I can agree with him because I've felt so much better physically and psychologically. My mediumship hasn't gone; it happens spontaneously and I still use it but, for now, I've decided to live a normal life as best I can and my health is improving tremendously.

When working, it's not healthy to become too focused on the spirit world. You can become so tied up in doing talks and workshops and demonstrations that you become oblivious to the practical realities of life. My husband and children certainly deserve gold stars for putting up with my state of mind all those years.

Also, it stands to reason that if you're taking on the persona of different spirits all the time, your own self can get lost. This gets dangerous if you begin to find it difficult to distinguish between what's real and what isn't. When there's a complete breakdown with reality, then madness and psychosis can be the result.

Other problems that seem to go with mediumship are related to the ego. Some mediums act as if they're on a special mission; they get a kind of messiah complex, or else become dogmatic and ego-bound. I've known many mediums who thought that they were above everyone else, and would throw terrible tantrums and take offence at the slightest thing. I know I've done that in the past. I'd like to think it was due to sensitivity because I had seen too many people who thought they were all-powerful. I was consciously aware that I didn't want to go down that path myself.

I've also seen mediums treat students appallingly. I've seen them manipulate, lie and not be willing to accept they could possibly make a mistake in the way they work. All of which is ridiculous because we're all human and we all make mistakes.

If you're a medium you have to be alert to all of these problems, simply from a personal point of view. But you also have to be alert to how you're affecting others.

Mediumship carries a huge responsibility. To be truly of service to those on earth and to those in the spirit world, you need to have self-discipline, common sense, a stable personality, and compassion for others.

When people have just been bereaved, they're in great distress. I've said this before, but it bears repeating. They are vulnerable, needy and often very suggestible. Anything that you say to that person can have far-reaching consequences for him or her. So you have to be aware of everything that you say and do.

A medium needs to learn skills for dealing with people, just as a psychiatrist or priest or doctor does. You need to understand the workings of the mind and be aware of psychological mechanisms such as projection and transference. You also need to respect confidentiality. You have to be able to deal with crisis situations. When giving workshops, for example, it's fairly common to have one or two people within the group who are quite unbalanced. This can sometimes present difficulties.

It helps enormously if you have someone you trust, who understands mediumship, to whom you can go for supervision and support. Ideally, you would also be continually doing work on yourself. Then you can understand your own motivations and emotions, and can work more honestly, effectively and compassionately with those who come to you for guidance.

I once overheard one of the students who'd refused to take a contact from me in a demonstration telling her friend afterwards that she didn't want to encourage me because I was too good. So finally, in addition to your need to protect others, you need to be able to protect yourself – not from the spirit world, but from the negativity on earth, including the Green Eye of envy.

CHAPTER SEVEN

The Principles of Spiritualism

The Seven Principles of Spiritualism were given to the medium Emma Hardinge Britten, in a message from the great Socialist reformer, Robert Owen.

In 1890, she set up the Spiritualists' National Union to unite all the different Spiritualist Churches and to advance the philosophy of Spiritualism contained in the Seven Principles. But it was not until the 1950s that Spiritualism was accepted as a religion.

The Seven Principles of Spiritualism, in modern language, are:

- **The Fatherhood of God.** The universe is created and orchestrated by Mind, or God.
- **The Brotherhood of Man.** Although there are inequalities as we travel along our individual soul's path, at the final stage we are all ultimately equal.
- **The Communion of Spirits and the Ministry of Angels.** Through our minds, we can communicate with the world of spirit. We all have helpers or guides in the spirit world.
- **The continuous existence of every soul.** Our soul is eternal. The existence and identity of the individual continues after the transition we call physical death.
- **Personal responsibility.** The mind is responsible for its own actions, so only we ourselves can take the blame for our mistakes and the credit for our successes. Everything that we think, do, or say is our own responsibility.
- **Compensation or retribution for good or evil deeds.** We reap what we sow. At some point in time, we will be our own judge. For every evil or destructive action, word or thought, recompense must be made.
- **Eternal progress open to every soul.** We are all redeemable.

The possibility of learning is open to all of us. We always have
the opportunity to progress to higher planes.

People often think that if you are a spiritualist, you are automatically a medium. In fact, a spiritualist is simply someone who subscribes
to the principles of Spiritualism.

These principles hold a wonderful message: There is one God.
Everybody throughout the world is connected. There are angels.
There is no death. We're responsible for everything that we do. We
have to live out the consequences of our own actions. Even when we
pass to the spirit world there is progress for everyone, however evil
they may have been.

The point is that spirits are still evolving. We might expect them to
be able to sort out our problems for us, or we might want a medium
to tell us what to do, but the spirit is the same after death as he was
the moment before. He hasn't evolved just because he no longer has
a physical body.

Of course, there are minds in the spirit world who are highly
evolved. They try to help and guide us personally, but they still hold
on to their own belief systems and they can't run our lives for us.
What they can do is to give us insight into our personal and spiritual
lives and help us to understand more about the spiritual beings that
we are.

Spiritualism was the only religion that made sense to me because it
was putting the onus on myself. Of the seven principles, personal
responsibility is the really big one. If we truly take this on board, we
have to constantly look at what we're doing and not blame others for
anything.

And that's hard. Taking responsibility for myself has not been very
pleasant at times. If there's anyone reading this book that I've upset,
I apologise now.

Having stopped work, I sometimes look back and think, heavens,
I was an absolute cow then! I was so volatile. Working all the time
with the root chakra brings up a lot of anger, and it wouldn't take much
to light the blue touch-paper. Since I've retired, I've become a much

calmer person and I'm happy to say the touch-paper is much longer now.

The problem with the Spiritualist Principles, just as with any other belief system, is that they are open to a wide variety of interpretations, and everyone has a different viewpoint. We have to take responsibility for everything we say and do, and also everything we think because, although we may not realise it, thought can affect what happens – to us and to other people.

Val, the friend I mentioned earlier, was absolutely seething when her ex-boyfriend took another woman skiing. All the time they were away, she sat there thinking, 'I wish she'd break her leg.' Val was made painfully aware of the power of thought when the woman did actually come back with a broken leg.

There are times when anger is appropriate. Not every little conflict or burst of anger needs a post-mortem. But when we have grievances that we keep building up, or when we project our own feelings onto someone else when we're really at fault, anger can be very destructive. Often our gut feeling tells us when we're doing that, though we may not listen to it.

I've always believed that no one else can forgive me for what I've done. I might apologise for something and they might say, that's ok, but that's not enough. I had to learn to forgive myself.

In Spiritualism, a great deal of emphasis is placed on philosophy. There were one or two mediums whose forte was philosophy, for example Jean Bassett, who lives in London and is a minister of the SNU. To listen to her was awe-inspiring, as she would be able to draw close to higher energies and work with highly evolved spirit guides.

Once, I had to work with mediumship after she'd finished her philosophy. Stepping onto the platform, the vibration I felt was of such a high level that it was incredibly difficult to bring it down to the type of energy I needed to be able to work with Mums and Dads and Auntie Flo. But it gave a good example of the different energies we use working with philosophy as opposed to mediumship.

On one occasion, I was giving a talk when I was overshadowed by a spirit who was talking through me. It was Robert Owen, a personal hero of mine, and the talk went like a dream.

Clearly, there are times when the medium does truly inspire those who are listening, but I'm afraid some of the philosophy that's channelled leaves much to be desired.

The President of Sutton Coldfield Church once said to me, 'We never hear any new philosophy.' I said, 'Well, what are we doing with the old?'

It's easy to complain that the philosophy always has the same message when we're still not loving our neighbour as ourselves! Of course, in order to do that, we have to know ourselves, and many people simply don't want to do the necessary personal work.

I really believed in the message that Spiritualism had to give – and still do. But within the Spiritualist Church, too much emphasis was placed on mediumship, and too little on the principles of Spiritualism. Spiritualism is a philosophy, the best one I've ever found. But the vast majority of people within Spiritualism, and certainly the committees of many churches, do not put that philosophy into practice. That's sad, because it will turn many people away from what I believe to be the greatest belief system that exists.

The longer I was associated with the Spiritualist Church, the more I became aware that the Church was simply not practising what it preached. In fact many people were clearly just intent on attacking or undermining the self-confidence of anyone who didn't do things the way they wanted them done.

I remember there was one particularly critical and arrogant medium who had been instrumental in giving at least two mediums nervous breakdowns. He'd been ousted as President of the Church where I was demonstrating and, on one occasion, he came into the service and started making notes and shaking his head and tutting while I was working. The chairperson was terrified; surreptitiously, she asked me if I was being assessed. I told her no, but he sat there through the whole thing, a sour expression on his face, scribbling away in his notebook. Then he got up and walked out before the collection.

A long time later this man sat behind me in a lecture at the College.

I was no longer going to let him rattle me. As soon as he sat down my protective wolf appeared, defending me against his negativity. I turned around after a while and saw that there was an enormous brown bear, another of my power animals, standing behind me. I relaxed completely. After the lecture, he walked up to me to say hello and shake my hand. Well, he'd never even spoken to me before, so I walked straight past him. I wasn't going to play his games.

It was interesting that something had shifted in him because something had shifted in me; he obviously sensed that I was no longer prepared to let him bully me. But it shook me when I realised I'd acted in a way that I wasn't proud of.

By that time I had become disillusioned with the SNU. It seemed to me to adhere too much to the old Victorian view of Spiritualism and not move on with the times. There was so much envy and jealousy; so many ego battles and people fighting for power. But even then it took me three years to pull away.

Finally I did, and for the last few years the only public demonstrations I did were for charity.

I had always enjoyed doing such demonstrations. One day my spirit guide San Lo said, 'We want you to do work for charity.' It was as simple as that.

'Ok,' I said, 'if that's what you want, I'll do it.'

I carried on working occasionally for local charities. Then a few months later Spiritualist Aid was started within the Spiritualists' National Union in order to raise money for charities both at home and abroad. When I became chairman, some months later, I devoted most of my time to it.

For me it was just a way of giving back. It also brought me more joy than anything else I'd ever done, because it was not just helping spirit and bringing comfort to people here, but also helping on a practical level in a broader field. San Lo said to me; 'Healing thoughts are all very well but these people need money too.' A lot of the money was sent to Croatia via the International Children's Medical Aid, a wonderful team of volunteers in London led by a lovely man called Peter Kingsley-Ducane who took convoys of drugs and food over to children both there and in Romania. He was very ill himself. But it didn't stop him giving his all to help them.

Four years ago I went to Zagreb in Croatia and saw the terrible conditions that children were being kept in. I remember hearing of a young girl who had cancer of the skin who was suffering terrible pain. There was no treatment, there were no drugs, they didn't even have an Aspirin. It made me aware how grateful I should be that I could go to a doctor freely and get whatever treatment I needed.

For so many people it's all just me and mine, they don't want to help anyone else. We should *all* be doing something to help.

CHAPTER EIGHT

Mediumship and Spirituality: Questions and Answers

Chapter Outline

When did mediumship begin?

Do you have to believe in God to be a medium?

What is the soul?

Do you believe in reincarnation?

Have you ever experienced anything that you couldn't explain?

Are there other worlds beyond our life on earth and the spirit world?

Have you experienced non-human intelligences or realms beyond?

What is spiritual healing?

Can we send healing energy to the earth?

When did mediumship begin?

Throughout history, people have been fascinated by mediumship and psychic phenomena. There are reports of mediumship in the earliest documents that exist. In fact, the Bible makes many references to the spirit world and to mediumship.

We know that Jesus was an outstanding medium and healer, and it may be that His materialisation after death was brought about through

His disciples' mediumship. It's well-known that with materialisation, someone from the spirit world feels as solid as you or I, and then the spirit disappears into the mist.

Throughout the ages, certain spirits, such as Jesus, Buddha, Mohammed, and other great prophets, have chosen to incarnate because they wanted to help mankind. They wanted to give us a message. Their words may be different, but their basic philosophies all run along similar lines.

Mankind then picks up these prophets and puts them on a pedestal, and we call ourselves Christians, or Buddhists or Muslims. Yet rather than all simply living in the way that these great spiritual leaders advised us to live, we use these distinctions to cause yet more conflict and divisiveness.

How many more prophets and great masters do there have to be for mankind to wake up to the simple message that has been given for thousands of years? If we all followed that message, it would be possible for wars to end; we could see all those millions of people dying of poverty and starvation truly as our brothers rather than just put fifty pence in a collection box and feel that we've done enough. We would be able to truly live in love.

Jesus's message was simply to be loving, caring, and faithful; to treat everyone as a brother and to treat others as you would like to be treated. Yet this message was manipulated by the church at the time simply in order to give it more power. It has been systematically undermined by the rules, dogma and politics of the Church ever since.

It has taken people a long time to realise that governments and institutions have no monopoly on – or even interest in – true spirituality. And all the while, there has been intense and repeated attack on any individuals or groups who have had the courage to oppose the established rule-makers.

Throughout history, the Law and the Church have persecuted mediums. Literally millions of women were burned at the stake as witches, and it's certain that a fair proportion of these were healers, psychics, mediums, or their sympathisers.

The 1735 Witchcraft Act was used to prosecute mediums. It

continued on the statute books right up until the middle of the twentieth century when it was repealed and replaced by the Fraudulent Mediums Act of 1951. Later, in the 1950s, Spiritualism was finally accepted as a religion.

In 1937 a working party was set up, led by Archbishop Lang, to investigate Spiritualism. This led two years later to the Church of England Report on Spiritualism. This acknowledged that mediumship gave evidence of life after death and communication with spirit. However, the report was not published until decades later. So, from a practical point of view, the beliefs of Spiritualism were no closer to being incorporated into the Church than they had ever been.

The legislation of 1977 states that it is illegal to make any diagnosis unless you are a doctor. It is forbidden to give spiritual healing to persons under sixteen years of age, to pregnant women, to patients with certain contagious or communicable diseases, for example sexually transmitted diseases, or to dental patients.

In recent times, more and more people have rejected organised religion. Many people today are seeking something other than rules and dogma; they're seeking a spiritual pathway, but are not sure where to find it. There is a void within them which, as always, makes them vulnerable to exploitation. Various 'gurus' spring up from time to time with various odd-brain ideas, and people follow them because they don't yet realise that the truth lies within themselves.

In the end, I don't think anyone has the answer for anyone else. The reality is that we must each find our own.

Do you have to believe in God to be a medium?

No, but it helps!

When we ask ourselves what God actually means, I think that everybody has a different perception of the answer. My personal view is that God is a power that we don't know much about. Nobody knows how life was created; we might think we know, but we don't. We're finding out new things about the universe every day. But the whole of existence is so immense that we can't even start to comprehend it.

God to me is compassion, love, and faithfulness to your convictions and to mankind. Simply put, you speak honestly and try not to hurt people.

The Dalai Lama defined his religion as kindness. I think if everyone took that view, then the world certainly wouldn't be in the state that it is in.

I don't believe in God in a human form. I think that man has always had a need for a superior power that he could personify as a god. Maybe that was the only way that our forefathers could conceive of the inconceivable.

What is the soul?

There is a general belief that we have a soul, and within the soul is that spark of spirit that gives us life and energy. The soul also contains a blueprint of who we are and what our life on earth is about. When the soul travels to the next world, it carries memories of things that we may regret as well as things that we found very joyful.

Gradually, the soul travels through many levels of consciousness, until what is left is pure spirit, and that will join with the energy of other spirits on its way to the God force.

From working with many different types of people, I know that there are some who have an inkling of having come from a place other than planet earth. They may get laughed at, yet all is possible. I believe that there are people on earth, not necessarily reincarnated, who have come here to try to help the planet and mankind from the catastrophic course that we seem to be on.

Such people are at times in total despair at having to live on this planet. They may have always felt completely alone in this world; although happy in their personal lives and relationships, there is a deep sense of being alone and not belonging, of looking into the sky at times and thinking, 'I want to go home.' Their auric fields are full of silver and blue and purple, and I believe these people have chosen to come back to earth to help others. To them, the world seems so cruel, people seem so unfeeling, their hearts break for all the starving children and cruelty and wars, and they have returned because they have a spiritual role to play on earth in helping people to overcome negativity and to become more compassionate.

These people may have had such thoughts themselves at times, but haven't really known what they meant. They need not be mediums or healers, yet in their very being they emit peace and bring light to this earth. In other words, they have some of the qualities that we normally ascribe to Jesus. So I believe it's possible that people from the higher realms of the spirit world, who have true compassion and caring, incarnate in order to try to raise the vibration on earth. By simply being, they are helping to bring light to earth.

There is a battle going on, in the heavens as well as on earth, between good and evil; between love and compassion on the one hand and negativity and destructiveness on the other. One of the reasons that any of us can be pulled down in the way we feel is that we are surrounded by negativity all the time. The world is full of conflict: wars and political struggles, famines and disasters. Newspapers, TV programmes, and even films, can have a negative effect on us. We have to rise above this negativity to find a positive approach to life. And it really is a battle.

Some people spend their life trying to bring justice to those who are exploited, just as others spend their life trying to bring in the spiritual light. As we break away from the old concepts of religion and God, I believe that more people will become aware of more than just material things, like making money and cleaning house, and will find their true purpose here on earth.

Do you believe in reincarnation?

You often hear people talk of youngsters as old souls, meaning that they have wisdom beyond their years, and I do think it's a possibility that some souls are reincarnated. There seems to be a great deal of evidence that some people have existed previously on earth in a past incarnation. I see no reason why, if we choose, we cannot be reincarnated. But I believe that we as spirit have free choice, and the idea that everyone reincarnates takes away that element of free choice.

I know that a lot of people have been told by mediums that the illnesses or problems that they are suffering are a result of something dreadful that they did in a previous life. It doesn't help anyone to be told that, and it can leave people with tremendous feelings of guilt. It also appears to presume some supreme being or wrathful God is punishing us. I have difficulty accepting that.

I remember years ago I went on a twenty-four-hour fast to raise money for famine victims in Africa, and somebody said to me, 'I won't give to that. I believe it's their karma to starve to death.'

I was really angry, and replied; 'Well, maybe it's my karma to try to help them.'

The idea of reincarnation has gained popularity in the West in recent times. Yet it's not at all clear to me what it's supposed to mean.

The classical idea of reincarnation originated in the East. In Hinduism, the atman is the part of us that reincarnates; it is impersonal and carries no personal memories or characteristics by which a given person could be identified. In Buddhism, if I understand it correctly, there is nothing personal that is transferred from one body to the next. In Taoism, there is continuity of existence but not of a personal self. In other words, the Western idea that 'I' was something in a past life is flawed in our very definition of the 'I' that was or is. If we can't pin down what it is that continues from one life to the next, then we are either being punished for someone else's bad deeds, or we are making excuses for not taking responsibility for our actions in the present. Either way, many Westerners are just using a word without understanding the concept contained within it.

It seems a much better idea to focus on what you're doing here and now, become aware of who you really are, and take responsibility for your failings and mistakes and credit for your strengths and successes. Personal responsibility is a straightforward and worthy goal that would keep most of us productively occupied for the whole of our lifetime. The idea that the soul of each of us exists before birth and survives after death does not need to be, and in fact is not, related at all to the concept of reincarnation.

The whole subject is so complex. We can have ideas about it but how can we know the true answer until we've experienced it ourselves? Even if we get information from a higher being in the spirit world, the information has to be limited to that soul's experiences. If you were asking a surgeon for an explanation about an operation, you'd get one version. Ask another, and he would give you a completely different version. Even in the spirit world there are limitations.

Many of us limit our ideas simply to what we can see and touch. Maybe we accept the spirit world as being a reality, but do we allow our thoughts to go to the vastness beyond that, where our spirit can exist on many different levels in many different places? I know it's not just a case of 'we're either here or we're in the spirit world.' There are so many other levels of existence. I don't just mean on planet earth but a whole realm of experience we're just not able to comprehend at the moment. I think it's certainly possible that we exist in another time and space at the same time as we exist here and that many, but not all, of our memories are erased.

I have experienced different places and different levels of consciousness. But I wouldn't fix this to an earth plane existence. Once, I was sitting down to prepare talks for a workshop when I suddenly felt, 'What on earth am I doing in this God-forsaken place?' I had memories of an orange sun and being in a very tranquil place. If our consciousness can create our surroundings and situations, then it doesn't necessarily have to mean that it is an as yet undiscovered planet. It could be a level of consciousness where people of like minds gather together to create that world.

Everything is so vast we can't even begin to imagine it. But if the majority of people shy away from the idea of an afterlife on this earth, anything beyond that is going to sound like sci-fi or comic-strip stuff to them!

I think we can learn from our experiences here. Hopefully, over time, we do evolve so that, as we get purer and purer, the pettiness and jealousy and rivalry are eventually non-existent. That pure state, when we have left our humanness behind, is when we truly evolve and experience other realms; when we make that beautiful journey back to that wonderful power that we call God.

It's an acknowledged scientific fact that physically the universe is constantly expanding. I believe that it's also constantly expanding in other ways and that it's through the power and the experiences of the collective consciousness that this expansion of the universe happens, rather than individual consciousness. It's certainly not just our experiences on earth.

Have you ever experienced anything that you couldn't explain?

In Spain a few years ago there was a spate of unexplained disappearances. An English diplomat went into the mountains with his wife. They got out of the car and he disappeared and was never seen again. His wife was distraught. She couldn't even get a pension as there was no death certificate.

When I was asked to help, I could sense him. Not on this earth, and not in the spirit world, but in some other realm of consciousness. I called in another medium as I couldn't get through to him. I felt this different energy. He was existing in some other dimension. He was not dead, not in the spirit world, but in another dimension entirely. My colleague confirmed what I'd felt, but neither of us was able to contact him.

My view is that if you close your mind to the possibility of the spirit world, then you also close your mind to any other possibilities. Our belief systems can be very restrictive. You have to have an open mind because, in the end, anything is possible. As Shakespeare so wisely put it, 'There are more things in Heaven and Earth, Horatio, than are dream'd of in your philosophy.' Finally, a closed mind leads to a closed life.

Are there other worlds beyond our life on earth and the spirit world?

Our consciousness can travel to many realms that are not just limited to the next world. We can travel and experience things that are not of this world, that are not human. We can travel to other places of existence, other parts of the universe. I don't see the realms as threatening. I have an enormous sense of wonder and excitement about all the other places I've experienced, where intelligence exists but not in a form that's the same as ours.

Norma, the friend I mentioned earlier who is mediumistic, had a very open mind and was always willing to just sit and see what happened. One day, while I was at her house we decided to sit for half an hour. Suddenly I was aware that I was in a different realm of consciousness. It felt completely different from either the spirit world or working with my guide or with healing energies.

There was a chamber without walls. It's hard to describe, but this chamber was full of the husks of human bodies. Thousands and thousands of them. I then sensed a shining light and, moving my consciousness towards that light, I became aware that I was now in the spirit world. The feeling was amazing. I wished I could have stayed there. It was totally filled with love and peace, and I felt completely at one with myself and the universe.

I don't know how long I stayed in that place but when my awareness came back, the feeling in the room had changed completely. Although Norma hadn't experienced the energies in the same way, she had shared some of the joy of the experience I'd had. She felt lighter and clearer, and she felt that the energy was something quite different.

When I was relating this story to a friend she said, 'That's interesting because the Hindus believe that we leave the bodies in such a place before the soul travels on.' So our own minds and the religious beliefs we hold will affect the way we enter the spirit world. For example, a Christian might expect to see Jesus, and a Hindu might expect to see the room of husks with the shining light. In the end, all ways lead to God; no way is greater or better than the next. When we are free of the physical body and the limitations of our conscious minds, we will be capable of exploring all these wonderful realms. I find this an extremely exciting prospect!

Already our minds can contact other worlds, which can seem a bit scary. But experiences such as these make me think, 'If I can do this now, what will I be able to do when I haven't got a physical body?' It's so exciting: the power of the mind is so immense. And most of the time we don't even realise what's possible. We write off such experiences as imagination or wishful thinking, yet the fact is that we have the power to create whole worlds within our minds. I believe that in years to come mankind will truly recognise the power of the mind.

As humans we have such unimaginable capabilities. We can see the spirit world. We can travel in our minds wherever we want to go, if we can only break out of the mind-set that tells us we're making it up or that such things are impossible. If we limit the mind only to what we know, if we're not willing to search for and accept other possibilities, then in reality we're only half alive.

If we can pass to the spirit world and feel content that we've tried not to hurt people, that we've done our best to overcome our problems, recognising our jealousy and bitterness, and not blaming other people for what we have suffered, then we will be in a state of heaven when we get to the other side.

Heaven and hell are simply a state of mind, both here and in the spirit world. We create Hell here on earth by filling our minds with negative thoughts, and if we hold on to that negativity, we're going to stay in exactly that same state when we pass. So there are lots of good reasons why we need to become more aware of what we are, and of how we are using our mental energy.

Have you experienced non-human intelligences or realms beyond?

Some years ago, I used to sit with a group for the development of mediumship, and to blend further with my guide, San Lo. The people in the group were all intelligent, thinking people who would always look further, and would not accept things unquestioningly.

After a while, we started to feel a different energy within the group. It was certainly not human, and it was not of the spirit world. There was no feeling of emotion attached to it at all. Everyone sensed it, and we all agreed that the closest description was of stainless steel.

They, whoever or whatever they were, said that the earth itself was sending out SOS messages to the universe, and that they were trying to help our planet.

This came as a bit of a shock! But it happened so often over a period of months that I had to accept that it wasn't just wishful thinking. When this energy appeared, the people in the group would all see a change in my face. It became quite angular, not at all the chubby double-chinned face that I've normally got.

We waited to see if anything would develop from these messages, and we never spoke of them to anyone outside the group. But the whole point of them seemed to be that we should be aware of the crisis that is approaching the earth; we should all be looking after the earth, and looking after each other.

Some time after this, I was doing a demonstration in a church in Droitwich Spa in Worcestershire. It was going quite well, with various contacts from the spirit world. Suddenly, from nowhere, I pointed to a lady in the congregation and said, 'You'll understand what I mean by stainless steel!' About an hour later it happened again. I pointed at another woman and said exactly the same thing.

Afterwards, both came to speak to me and broke down crying, saying, 'Thank goodness you've confirmed I'm not going mad!' While sitting for development, they'd both had similar experiences to me and were relieved to hear that they were not alone. Having open minds, they accepted that there must be realms of intelligences beyond our own, of which we have no idea.

Some time later, I met one of my ex-students from Sutton Coldfield Church, a young woman called Ruby. She said, 'Something really peculiar happened in meditation last week; I saw three figures, and all

I can say to you is they weren't of this earth. I heard the words, "Tell Sue Brotherton."'

Although I was astonished, I didn't want to tell her of my experiences in case it influenced what happened to her, so I told her to let me know if anything else happened. When I bumped into her a few weeks later, she said that she'd felt the same energy around her again, and that the best way she could describe it was like stainless steel.

People often call such beings aliens, and assume they want to attack us or kill us or take over the world. I'm certain that life is far more complex than we all imagine. I can quite happily accept that there are more highly evolved beings than us in the universe, who aren't interested in killing and wars, who want to help earth in whatever way they can. Their original home may not have been earth but that doesn't stop them wanting to help us. Looking at the way we're living our lives, the way we're damaging the earth for the minerals that it contains, polluting the seas, and destroying the forests, I sometimes fear that mankind won't wake up until it's too late.

The few people that do accept that we can communicate with levels of consciousness outside of human personalities are often thought to be off the wall, but, as a very down to earth person, I know that it happens and that life exists in this universe other than our own. Often as a group, we would be aware of tall, slender beings, not of this earth, and I just think we have to have a completely open mind. There's nothing to be afraid of. It's only when we close our mind and get bogged down in the mundane things of life that we stop being joyful and excited and open to new possibilities.

My dear friend Ann Anderton explained to me how astrologers describe the rotation of the earth in our solar system through our galaxy in terms of twelve periods of two thousand one hundred years, each named after the signs of the Zodiac. It is said that we are moving out of the Piscean Age that was characterised by authoritarian values, materialism and satisfaction of desires, hypocrisy, suffering and the pursuit of world unity by force. We are now moving into the Aquarian Age, which will be characterised by harmony, equality, healing, and the achievement of our spiritual potential.

I think it's going to take a while, but I do believe that a new consciousness will finally dawn, bringing more co-operation and understanding than the earth has ever known.

What is spiritual healing?

It's often said that spiritual healers are the unsung mediums, for they work tirelessly and faithfully, for no financial reward, to bring healing energies from the universe to people in need.

If any person has true compassion and love for other people, for animals and for the world, s/he can contact those energies and draw them close to earth. I do not believe that spiritual healing can be governed by man-made rules and regulations.

Within the myriad levels of consciousness that we inhabit, many different healing energies exist. A medium has to be in an altered state of consciousness in order to reach this energy, and every medium will feel it in a different way. When working with a spirit contact, the consciousness of the medium reaches out and meets with the consciousness of the person in spirit. While this is happening, the medium will often also see healing colours. For me the healing energy was often blue.

Watching spiritual healers at work, I could feel the power of the energy passing through them to the person receiving it. A healer's hands are often guided to certain areas of the person's body, which turn out to be where there is pain or discomfort. If the recipient has an accepting mind and is open and receptive, this aids the healing process, but this isn't necessary in order for the healing to work. There are many different forms of healing: Reiki, for example, is very popular. However, I believe that it is all the same energy. Different people just take different pathways to reach it.

I have seen a deaf woman get her hearing back after one session of healing.

Another wonderful example was an old lady whose heart was so bad that she couldn't walk more than ten feet without getting out of breath. Her healing took place over a period of a couple of years.

Shortly after it had finished, I attended her wedding where she happily danced the night away!

Recently in Spain, I started talking to a woman in a cafe in Fuengirola and the subject of healing came up. She said that she'd had rheumatism in her fingers for some time. So Dave, my husband who has been a healer for over twenty-five years, held her hand for a few minutes, gave her healing, and afterwards she said, 'It's unbelievable, the pain has gone!'

Healers will often attract the help of doctors in the spirit world. Although they are no longer in a physical body, these doctors still have a desire to help people overcome illness and they may specialise in certain complaints. There are one or two healers who act as psychic surgeons, and they perform operations that often look quite bizarre! I'm not sure that they actually need to work in this way, but I know from personal experience that it certainly does work at times. At other times, it's not so successful and I've no idea why this should be so.

When Steve Turoff first worked at Sutton Coldfield Church I attended one of his sessions of psychic surgery. Half way through I had to go to the bathroom. When I came back I could actually smell anaesthetic, although I knew for a fact that there was none in the room. Another medium who was present at the time, Gerard Smith, said that when he looked at Steve's hands, he could see a spirit's hands working there with him.

Sadly, many people accept only that which is visible and tangible. Believing in only one consciousness is like walking along a very narrow corridor; there's so much more to be discovered. Although a part of me is living on earth now, in a physical body, there are many other parts co-existing simultaneously. We're not just living one consciousness; our consciousness is immense and limitless. We can explore so many different realms now when we're here on earth as well as when we're on the other side.

Imagine your mind going up in a lift. When you're working with spirit, you might be getting out at the first floor. To reach the healing energies, you might have to go to the fourteenth floor, in which case the mind carries on beyond spirit contacts, continuing all the way up, to finally reach nothingness. I believe that when we are truly within the healing power, our consciousness is gone; we're not aware of ourselves, or of anything around us. That's the way it works for me anyway.

There have been times when I've been giving healing when I've actually seen the Good Shepherd, as I call Him. Jesus was one of the best healers of all time, and when I was in need of healing myself, I would find it much easier if I brought the image of the Good Shepherd to mind. It's something to fix the mind on, to help attune to the healing energy. For Western people, Christ is part of our belief system, whereas for people from the East it might be the Buddha appearing. I think anyone can bring healing to themselves if they sit quietly, perhaps with some relaxing music, and allow their mind to drift to a higher level. To picture a prophet that they have faith and belief in can help their mind to travel.

If you are feeling depressed or ill, you can sit for a few minutes seeing yourself bathed with a beautiful light, and a powerful healing can result. Or if there is someone you love that is suffering, you can imagine him in your mind, see yourself holding his hand and send him healing energy, bathing him in blue and purple or white light. Alternatively, to sit in a group where healing is taking place, without laying-on of hands, can be a very positive experience.

Can we send healing energy to the earth?

We can send healing energy to anyone, anywhere in the world. Years ago, there was a wonderful story about the Mods and Rockers when they were constantly at war with each other. On one particular day, there were rumours of a great clash coming and a convoy of Mods set out on their scooters on their way to Brighton. A healing group, worried what might happen, sent healing energy to them. Suddenly, without explanation, the Mods all turned round and went back home!

At the time of the racial riots in the Handsworth district of Birmingham, our group used to do a simple healing exercise. We would bring to mind the Post Office Tower, one of the tallest buildings in Birmingham. We would sit and visualise healing energy being sent out from the top of the Tower, extending outwards to cover the whole of the city and surrounding areas.

For many years at the end of any gathering I was involved with, we would use a similar exercise; after sending healing energy to our fellow man, we would send energy not just to our local area but also to the whole of the world. There are certainly groups of people all over the world who are doing exactly the same thing.

Some people will be sceptical, but maybe they don't appreciate the power of the mind and what we can create with it. If more people sent out positive thoughts and pure love and healing energy, we could do a lot to alter the state of the world, particularly if we form small groups of people to do it collectively.

Some of the most spiritual people I know have been sitting at home for years, simply sending absent healing to those who are sick and to problem areas in the world. If everybody did that just for a few minutes when they got into bed, if they used the power of their minds to send healing, it could bring about great changes in the way the world is today. Small effort by large numbers of people would certainly add up to something truly significant.

CHAPTER NINE

Working with Mind, Energy and Spirit

Chapter Outline

Levels of Consciousness

Projection and Personification

Transpersonal Work: Working with Sub-personalities

Psychic Work

Mediumistic Work

Levels of Consciousness

Brain wave studies, or EEGs, which record the electrical signals from the brain, show that different brain wave frequencies are associated with different levels of activity and states of awareness.

Beta waves, 14 to 20 Hz, are found in our normal waking state. Alpha waves, 8 to 13 Hz, occur in meditation or daydreaming. Theta waves, 4 to 7 Hz, are found in sleep and deep meditation. Delta waves, from 0.5 to 3 Hz, occur in deep sleep and profound meditative and healing states.

Fast brain waves, or Gamma rhythms, 20 to 100 Hz, occur following sensory stimulation, during both waking and dream states. They are involved in higher mental activity including perception and consciousness, and disappear during anaesthesia.

We know that there are many different levels of consciousness. But I don't think that the boundaries between them are as clear as might be suggested. I believe that there are levels other than those commonly defined. We can shift in and out of different states of consciousness, and they can sometimes overlap. Even when I'm talking about different levels of consciousness, my consciousness shifts and I talk in a way that I wouldn't normally. I remember things that my conscious mind would not normally have access to.

We know very little about the workings of the mind. The mind has immense uncharted potential, so it's very difficult to categorise all the possible states of awareness that we are capable of experiencing.

Our conscious minds contain just what we're conscious of at any point in time; the thoughts we're having, what we're planning to do tomorrow, and what's going on immediately around us. Our conscious mind is aware of just a small fraction of what we're actually sensing and experiencing from minute to minute.

The unconscious mind is much more alert to all the different sensations and inputs that we experience. Although we're not aware of it, we're learning all the time from what we see or sense or feel, and these impressions become stored in the unconscious mind in symbolic form. Everything that we have experienced through our lives – our thoughts, feelings and memories – is available within the unconscious mind. When we wish to access that information and learning, we can use various techniques to help it rise into consciousness.

Our unconscious mind uses symbols rather than words. I call these symbols the language of the soul. They come from the right side of the brain, the visual, imaginative, irrational side, more than from the verbal, rational, logical left side of the brain. The conscious mind tends to be dominated by the left side of the brain in normal waking consciousness, though clearly some people are more right-brained and more in touch with their intuitive side even whilst caught up in the mundane daily routine that takes up so much of our waking state. So we need to acknowledge that these symbols are important, and they do have meaning, as otherwise we tend to tend to dismiss them as rubbish and never take them seriously.

Once we start working with the images that come to help and guide us, and as we become more adept at drifting from one state of consciousness to another, we can begin an ongoing dialogue with our unconscious mind. This allows us to accept creative impressions and access inner knowledge. We can also find out much more about our own emotions, both positive and negative.

It's often the case that we're not consciously aware of many of our emotions. In our day-to-day lives, we spend a lot of energy trying to deny our feelings. We don't spend enough time listening to them, trying to work out what they're about – or even allowing ourselves to find out what they actually feel like. Unless we know what jealousy feels like, how do we know we don't get jealous? Our left brain says, 'I don't get jealous,' because it hasn't even given that right brain feeling a name.

We're scared of feelings, especially negative ones, yet the greatest help comes when we're no longer afraid to look at them and own them as ours. Once we know what a particular emotion feels like, we can recognise it. Admitting it and acknowledging it takes power away from that feeling, whereas while we're denying it all the time it actually gains power. To feel jealous or envious or angry are all perfectly natural human functions. They only become problems when we don't see them for what they are. All of us need to let a bit more sunlight shine on the negativity that we carry within ourselves.

We can all become more in tune with our intuitive side. The unconscious mind communicates spontaneously with us through our dreams, imagination, intuition and creativity. When the conscious mind has relaxed its hold over us, such as in dreaming or meditation or trance, we can see things from a different perspective, and we're more receptive to new ideas. It's well documented that many great inventions and ideas have been discovered during sleep. We can also experience the spirit world more easily because the natural boundary between the two worlds is much thinner. People often report dreaming of loved ones in spirit.

Our conscious awareness is so small if you look at the vastness of the total consciousness that we are. We all have a spiritual level to our being. We can all access the vast area of our unconscious mind, that deeper level of consciousness from where our symbols come. The more we do this, the more the knowledge that exists in the unconscious self starts to rise into the awareness of the conscious mind.

When working, I used to do a lot of inspirational talks. I would also be constantly planning workshops, as I had to keep finding different themes to inspire the students to work. Often, I would get up early in the morning, sit at the computer and it would just flow out, before my left brain had time to wake up properly. I'd see an image and suddenly get a rush of thoughts. Yet if I had to think while doing a workshop, I wouldn't be able to. I would prepare an outline beforehand of what I wanted to say, but it would come intuitively at the time; the work with that group would be purely inspirational, from my own creative being.

I think that our own creative being, our own spirit, is of equal value to those in the spirit world and, while we have spirit guides who will help us, we all also have that inner guidance, the higher self, or intuitive mind. When we alter our consciousness, we're altering our own vibration, and this makes it easier to make contact with those in the spirit world who are helping us or wanting to guide us. But it also makes it easier to listen to our own intuitive mind. In fact, when we start to access this knowledge and information from the higher self, a change in consciousness automatically happens. This facilitates guidance from the spirit world at the same time, so that the two become intertwined, and we receive help both from our higher selves and from above.

To open the door to our creative self, we need to give ourselves quiet time in which to learn the language of our intuitive mind. These days we want everything to be a quick fix, for example, with the TV, the Internet, and fast food. We always want things to arrive instantly so we rarely allow ourselves to quietly sit and listen to our own thoughts, or write a journal, or jot down our dreams.

I was doing a workshop in Spain several years ago on the Shadow Self. A Norwegian man said to me, 'I haven't got a shadow side any more, I did a weekend workshop on it.' Other people try doing mind exercises for two or three days and then when they haven't felt any results, they discard them. The point is that no one has a magic wand; to make changes and gain insights into yourself and the workings of your mind and emotions takes time, there are no short cuts. We expect to be able to contact our higher selves or to contact spirit in three easy steps, but I think it's a lifetime's work.

To find gold we have to dig deep. We can find little nuggets quite easily, feel happy with them and think we've done enough, but the real gold is hidden deep within ourselves. It's backbreaking work at times, and often we just want to down tools and rest and not go back to work at all.

But the fact is that in order to find the real joy, the real contentment that is our birthright, we have to do a lot of digging.

The enlightened ones are people who have an open mind; their minds aren't closed off at all. They can travel with the mind and experience many different levels of being. Of course, a lot of them are labelled mad, but gradually things are changing.

It has always been difficult to prove mediumship, because you can't guarantee it will happen in a certain way, but quantum physics has at last confirmed what simple-minded mediums have been saying for years. If you were in the spirit world you could just walk through a table. We now know scientifically that that table only feels solid because it's vibrating at a certain frequency. Even a lot of the science fiction of forty years ago is now accepted as fact. And there is still so much that we don't know.

Trying to put labels on things that are invisible and unprovable is very difficult. The categories defining different mind states or levels of consciousness are not distinct.

I believe that we all have a spirit, the spark of life that is simply energy. We also have a Higher Self, which is our guiding wisdom, or intuitive knowledge, that can help us on our spiritual journey. And we have an unconscious mind that holds personal knowledge at a deep level of consciousness, and also contains collective and spiritual knowledge. There are so many levels of consciousness, all of which are linked, with no strict line of demarcation between them.

Each one of us has a vast consciousness, so vast that we can't even imagine it. Our own universe. We are able to access all levels of spirituality ourselves, without an intermediary, from the healing levels to the philosophy of the great masters. There are so many levels of consciousness we can take our mind to. But, just as we resist the realisation that we are spirit, we resist even more the idea that the shadow side exists within us too, at the depths of our very being. We are the light and the shadow.

If we travel to the spirit realms, we also have to travel within our own being and look at the things that are holding us back and stopping us from being a whole person. If we go on this double journey, it can change our auric field to the extent that we are then able to help other people. After all, if you can't understand yourself then how can you expect to help or understand anyone else?

If we're brave enough to go on that journey, we don't judge people as harshly as we would do otherwise. There's an old Sioux saying that says, 'Never judge another until you have walked in his moccasins for thirty suns and thirty moons.' We criticise in others the traits that we possess ourselves, and if we don't do our own personal work then all we do is project our own negative feelings onto others and act as if there's nothing wrong with us. We exist in a state of denial rather than trying to rectify our faults and mistakes.

I believe that when we pass into the spirit world it's not God that will judge us. It's our own unconscious mind, our own consciousness, which we have to face.

I've seen people with all the wealth and power imaginable that others might envy, and I realised a long time ago that these worldly things do not necessarily bring contentment. On the other hand, I've also seen people who have literally nothing. Yet they do have peace and contentment, they really do treat others as their brother.

Our life should be about exploring who we really are in order that we can live at peace with ourselves and our fellow men. Then, when we pass to the spirit world, I believe that our minds will eventually be free of the heavy burden of negativity and self-denial. We will indeed be in, or be able to reach, a state of heaven or nirvana.

One of the hardest things is to admit any fault on our own part and to say sorry. It is a great sadness that so many of us will not even attempt to follow the greatest journey that we can have, which is to know and accept who and what we are.

Projection and Personification

A psychiatrist, a psychic and a medium can all tell people things that they – at some level – already know. A psychiatrist might do this by simply observing them, listening to what they talk about and noticing how they respond to certain questions. A psychic might sense their energy field, and travel into their subconscious mind. A medium might do all of these things, but also tell them things they didn't know, because s/he is able to obtain information from the spirit world. It's this capacity to link with the spirit world that means that only a medium can give proof of life after death.

The point is that there are many different levels of consciousness. When mediums are tuning in to a person here on earth, they feel different vibrations as they travel through the different parts of that person's psyche. There are often areas of heavy, dense energy that feel completely different to the light champagne feeling of the spirit world.

Only it's not always that easy. Some mediums can pick up on different levels of consciousness, but they may not be aware of the mechanics of what they're doing, or be able to distinguish between the different levels. They sense someone and may be able to describe that person, his characteristics and feelings. They assume it's a spirit, when in fact it's not. It is a part, or sub-personality, of the person they're working with.

They're actually tuning in to the psyche of the person in front of them rather than to the spirit world, yet they give the reading as if they have contacted a spirit. The person can sometimes link the information in to someone s/he knew, but more likely would not be able to recognise that contact at all. Naturally enough, as the 'spirit' being described is actually a dissociated part of themselves that they were not previously in touch with.

For example, let's imagine I am giving you a reading. You are sitting there, hoping I will contact your father who died six months ago. You are thinking of your father, you have an image of him in your mind and a record of him in your auric field. I, being psychic, can see both of these. I can draw a picture of him – his personality and characteristics, and even the things you might want him to say to you – straight out of your energy system or your subconscious mind.

It's a fact that all of us internalise, or introject, an idea, image, or part of each of the people who have been close to us. So that in effect certain aspects of those people become a part of ourself. Which we may or may not want to see.

Let's imagine that you were afraid of your father when he was alive. So now, whenever you feel afraid, you access the emotions or memory state of the times when your father was standing angrily in front of you. Your boss tells you off at work, and you see your father. Or, more likely, you've blocked out the fear that you felt in relation to your father because it was so unpleasant. When you're criticised by your boss, you feel a disproportionate amount of fear, and without realising where most of that fear originated, you automatically attribute it all to your boss. In fact, he was only the trigger.

This process is called projection, and we all do it.

Sometimes, when we're stressed or feeling down, we feel a fear for no apparent reason. Something we're unaware of has triggered a feeling deep inside us, the origins of which we're also unaware of. It's a bit like someone sneaking in and hitting you on the nose with a bamboo stick while you're snoozing. How confusing is that!

Now, when I tune into you, I feel that fear, and when I go deeper into that fear I see an image of your father. That's because whatever fear or feeling or sub-personality you are in the grip of at that moment can be projected, or personified, into human form. And when I tap into it, I *see* that human form.

What I'm actually seeing is a projection of an aspect of your own self. But if I don't fully understand the workings of the human psyche, I'm probably going to say I have your father here in spirit, and start trying to give you a message from him.

Transpersonal Work: Working with Sub-personalities

I used to give a lot of transpersonal sittings in which I would be primarily working psychically with aspects of the person's unconscious mind.

When we're stressed we put a barrier around ourselves. Some people have been so badly hurt by life's experiences that they've built up a very strong protection around themselves. Although consciously they may trust you and want to work with you, at an unconscious level they don't want to let you in. In fact, that protection could be part of the problems they're having in life, in getting on with people or finding a partner whom they can trust.

When I travelled into their subconscious mind, I would often be going down steps to some sort of courtyard. Archetypal images would then start appearing. There might be a robed figure waiting to meet me who would take me down more steps to a dungeon or a cave. There was often someone down there guarding the entrance.

Sometimes there would be a long corridor with doors on either side; many were shut but one would be open. When I went into that room, or cell, I would meet an aspect of the person's personality that wasn't being used. It had been hidden away or forgotten.

I would tell them which part they had lost. For instance, their inner strength might appear as a warrior or knight. I might see joy as a small child who, instead of being able to play happily, is neglected and chained up in a dungeon. People would always recognise this lost part of themselves, and might even remember when it was lost.

By finding it and acknowledging it, that sub-part could come forward to be freed; sometimes it was joy or creativity or self-confidence, something that the person desperately needed to integrate into themselves.

I would give people mind exercises, often visualisations, to do after the session, so that they could practise opening up to that part of them and integrating it consciously. These exercises were very effective in helping to bring about positive changes in their lives.

But sometimes they wouldn't do them. Although they wanted things to change, they weren't prepared to put in the work that would help to bring about those changes. I could only do so much for them; the rest was up to them. There were other people who wouldn't let me in to their subconscious mind at all. Many people are very private, or seek to avoid issues, or they don't want to continue when they realise they too are going to have to work.

In one sitting, I was travelling into a woman's subconscious mind. I was in a cave going down a dark tunnel. For many of us, there's a part of us that is undermining or destroying our life, and yet it will defend itself to the last. I got the sense that I was just about to meet that part of her.

Suddenly an enormous maggot filled the dark end of the tunnel. It was revolting, completely gross, writhing around right in front of me. I can tell you, you have to have your own internal warrior at the ready to cope with images like that! So I got out my sword and lashed into the maggot. It wasn't easy. It was a real slippery customer and it kept on hiding. It was so repulsive that there was a part of me that just wanted to leave it there and get out quick. But, prepared with my mind tools, I went after it, found it, and finally slayed it. In that case, the maggot represented lack of self-respect. After the session, the woman worked hard at the mind exercises that her unconscious mind had shown me. Her life suddenly changed, and she found that she could laugh again.

Often, a part of the person's subconscious defence system would attack me, not wanting to give up its power. I would meet huge, ferocious lions or God knows what. So working in this way can be very hard work and very tiring. The transpersonal approach works well with people who are creative and sensitive, as they can relate to the images that I draw from their unconscious mind, and can understand when I explain what those images represent. When told to do mind exercises afterwards, they are also more likely to do so.

I'll give an example of the whole process. Working with Teresa, I'm going to travel through her psyche now.

'As I'm blending with you, I feel that one of the problems you have is that you do not feel good enough; there are self-doubts. I'm actually seeing this as a werewolf standing by you, towering above you.' (Teresa: 'Yes, I've always been afraid of werewolves.')

'As I blend deeper into your unconscious mind, I'm seeking your inner strength, or protector, because I know they're there somewhere. Ah, there he is, an enormous tiger, I can feel his energy, he's very powerful, very strong. But as he leans against you, he's like a big pussycat, purring, and rubbing his head over your shoulders. The tiger is a part of you, your protector, who is here to help you slay this werewolf, to help you to overcome the self-doubts that have always been with you. When the self-doubts and negative thoughts come, bring the tiger to your mind, feel his strength.' (Teresa: 'Yes, I can feel that. I like that image.')

'The animal is instinct, it's not mind. A lot of mind is steeped in the logical stuff, so look for the instincts and characteristics, the loving and protective tiger, and use whatever comes into your mind. When you need to go somewhere such as the dentist, or an interview you're a bit nervous about, send your tiger ahead of you. If you get nervous at night, with your mind place him outside your door, and in your bedroom. What you're actually doing is strengthening your auric field so that you do not feel vulnerable to the outside world, as well as taking the power away from your self-doubts.

'Post the tiger around the house to protect the house and you. Have him here on the bed, at the door, in a number of places, between you and people who are negative towards you, and you may then find their attitudes change towards you.' (Teresa: 'Yes, I'll do that, I can see how that could work.')

'I'm still looking for the inner strength. I need to find the image that you can relate to, to bring that energy in and integrate it, and stop the negativity from interfering and draining your energy.' (Teresa: 'Yes, I feel when that drain of energy is happening.')

'Ah, here he is, I see him now. Yes, there's a Native American archetypal image there, and a maiden, dressed beautifully in a luminescent white-blue dress, with long red hair, very feminine. She's just standing there as if lost; an innocent, feminine part that's never been fully integrated.' (Teresa: 'I know I need to work with that.')

'And the inner strength, the Native American brave, bare-chested, barefoot, wearing buckskin trousers, with arrows on his back, and one white line painted over his nose; he's reaching out to this female, taking her by the hand and leading her to a brown and white horse; he's rescuing that lost part.

'They're on a mountain-top, and down in the valley there's a town; the girl wants to stay on top of the mountain, she's reluctant to go into the town. (Teresa: 'Yes, that's me all over.') The brave is encouraging her to overcome her fears. He is handsome, with dark hair braided at the back, a feather above his right ear, a medallion with feathers hanging down. He has a little dagger, and he's so strong. He's the rescuer, the inner warrior.' (Teresa: 'I feel comfortable with him. I know I need him to be around more.')

'The tiger and the brave are tools for you to use in dealing with the negativity, the demons that bother you. There are a couple of other demons eating away at you; they're not showing themselves, but they're sapping you of your energy. This could be creative energy, and also the inability to give yourself 110% to anyone. We'll look at those later.

'So that you can integrate this strength and power into your psyche, you can do a simple mind exercise. In the shower every morning, bring the picture of the brave to your mind, step into the skin of the brave as if you are putting on a glove. The picture may change of what he's wearing. You may find yourself going on the journey with him on the horse, and you'll find that you have the strength to go into situations you're afraid of. Fear has held you back, and opportunities have arisen that you haven't pursued.' (Teresa: 'Yes, I know that's true.')

'This man has a lot of integrity; he can give you the wings to fly. He has a bow and arrow, but he's not a warrior as such, he's like a young medicine man. He's saying that your role is about communication, messages; they seem to be messages of hope and of healing.' (Teresa: 'That's a lovely image. I like him. It's almost as if I can feel his strength just talking about him.')

'And remember that he represents your inner strength. We all lose our inner strength at times. We give our power away to situations and other people. But now you know how to reclaim your power.

'You may see an object you like that forms a connection to the warrior. In times of struggle, holding this talisman will give you immediate access to the strength and the power that is in you and helps to integrate them into your psyche. Once you start reclaiming them, these different aspects of yourself arrive when needed. You don't have to summon them up. And other people will respond to that energy.

'We have so many tools in our subconscious mind that we can use to overcome fears. The best time to bring the image of the warrior to mind is as soon as you recognise those doubts and fears coming into your mind. The more you work with these images, the easier it becomes, until in the end it's simply a quick picture in your mind and you can instantly feel the difference.

'Now this is brilliant, I can see the magician. That means transformation. He is holding out his hand to you. And that's wonderful, because I don't normally see the magician unless transformation is about to take place. So you'd better get working!'

(Teresa: 'Yes, I can relate to those images. Thank you, I promise I will work with them. I feel really excited.')

Everyone has their own personal symbols although they're often shown in archetypal forms such as the Warrior, Merlin the Magician, the Maiden locked away in the tower. But some people may be able to relate better to modern-day images.

For example, I sometimes used TV soaps, such as 'Coronation Street,' to explain how the archetypal images work. If I said, 'I can see someone, a real Mavis type, a ditherer, who's always indecisive,' people could identify with her, and start telling her to sod off when she'd pop up. Soaps contain all the archetypal figures, like the down-trodden husband, or the siren, and they have excellent characterisations that people can relate to because they're parts of themselves. When you know exactly which aspect of you is causing you problems, you can deal with it much more easily, so it is a good tool for everyday people to identify what is going on within themselves.

Usually, when working psychically with symbols from people's subconscious mind, one negative aspect comes to the fore. When they've dealt with that aspect, it frees them up and the stranglehold of that negativity is broken.

Transpersonal psychology involves people using what they see in a meditation, a dream, or a waking image, and working on it themselves. In my work, however, the images present themselves to me. I use my clairsentient ability to blend with them to feel what characteristics and emotions they represent. I draw out the images that are relevant to that individual person, which s/he can then later work with.

Many psychics don't deal with that aspect of the work. They're basically just feeding back to us the things that we would like to see happen. They're not helping us to understand how all the different parts of ourselves interact. They're not showing us how we can give energy to those positive parts we want to develop and take energy away from the parts that are undermining or draining us.

The most important thing for me was to be asking questions, learning, understanding more about myself, and being constantly aware that things are not always what they seem. So, throughout the years that I was working with the spirit world, I was also continually working on myself.

Most mediums don't do that.

Psychic Work

Our psychic ability is what we call the sixth sense; it helps us to survive. The more left-brained, rational and logical we are, the more we ignore our right-brained sensitivity and our gut feelings, which are the essence of our psychic abilities.

Working psychically, you can go into the mind of a person here, but not all psychics can go into the finer vibration of a person in spirit. Psychics can do much the same work as the medium, but they use material from the person's unconscious mind; they can give information about people who are dead, but it's not so specific and it won't be anything that the person doesn't know.

You can take the psychic work to a much deeper level if you understand about the human psyche and the language of the soul. Anyone who has worked with dreams will understand that each one of us has our own individual language, so that each person's symbols will have a different meaning.

In dream dictionaries, for example, you might read that a dog is supposed to mean friendship. But that cannot be so for everyone, as there are plenty of people to whom a dog brings terror. Everyone's dream language is specific and unique to that individual.

The unconscious mind contains many images and memories, much unprocessed knowledge that hasn't been translated into language. These images can be perceived by a medium, but the person him/herself then needs to interpret them in the context of his/her own experience. Instead of doing this, a medium will often say that the spirit world is working symbolically and go on to give messages that make no sense. I've checked with people who agreed that such a message made no sense to them, but they didn't like to say so in public in case it caused offence to the medium!

If mediums took the time to learn about the different levels of consciousness, and about the sub-personalities that exist inside all of us, they would realise that they are actually getting information about a person at a deep level of his own consciousness. By blending with the symbol, instead of assuming what it means, you can find out all about that person, and what they're going through emotionally. Then you travel through that level of consciousness and you can follow what their higher self is telling them. In this way you can help people to overcome the internal blocks that are holding them back in life.

If we don't know the difference between levels of consciousness, then everything will be put down to the spirit world. And that is just not true. The spirit world is one of intelligence. They don't give messages in gobbledygook. That's an insult, particularly if we are attributing those messages to a certain individual in the spirit world. Maybe they only wanted to say that they'd been with you, to let you know that they were close to you and had not deserted you.

So some of the messages I've heard mediums give are, in my opinion, insults to the intelligence.

Those in spirit are perfectly able to speak clearly, precisely and without ambiguity. They don't need to talk in riddles, and they don't use the type of personal symbols that come from someone's unconscious mind. So when I hear mediums say stuff like, 'He's giving me a glass of water now,' or 'She's tying a knot in a ribbon,' I tend to find myself feeling very irate. The medium is obviously not aware that all he's doing is reaching into the psyche of the person he's working with, bringing out a few personal symbols from the unconscious mind of that person, which he then hasn't a clue how to explain, and presenting it all as bona fide information from the spirit world.

Sidney Jourard said, 'Be careful in your choice of hypnotists.' Well, that goes for mediums too!

No medium I knew worked with symbols. In fact, I used to have many disagreements with a well-known medium, who stated that he never worked with symbols and didn't believe in the unconscious mind! I demonstrated with him on platform once. He was working with a woman in the audience. He said to her, 'He's saying you'll see a light in the form of a shell on a brick wall.' She shook her head, nonplussed, as it clearly had no meaning for her.

I tuned in to the symbol in her unconscious mind, and saw one of the shells with seven lines running down it. I blended with the image, and felt desperation, fear and loneliness, and I knew that the last seven years had been very difficult for that lady. The wall that the shell was hanging on was impenetrable, and I knew that she'd had to build up a wall around herself to protect against further pain. I didn't go any further than that, as I wasn't working with her, and I had to respect her privacy.

Another medium said of a contact in the spirit world, 'This man liked the sea, and he is showing me memories of when he went to a seaside place where the sea was very rough.' This was something that the woman's father in spirit was supposedly saying, yet she couldn't relate to it. In fact the medium was going into the woman's own unconscious emotions.

In this case, I would go into her unconscious mind and blend further with the image of the sea. Often I could actually count the waves, so I would know that she had gone through a difficult time emotionally for that number of years. If I had been working with her in private, I would then go beneath the waves and see what was on the bottom of the sea; there might be various objects, such as a wrecked car, rubbish, perhaps an old fridge. I would then see what was behind each of those objects; I would open the fridge and see what had been hiding in there, maybe something that had been frozen for a long time.

Travelling deeper into the stillness of the water, I would meet one of her sub-personalities, a part of her that could overcome some of the problems she had been facing, for example a deep-sea diver with an oxygen tank who was coming to help her. This would then be an image that she could later work with herself.

Travelling into a person's unconscious mind, I actually see the images and objects, whereas using mediumship I don't see things anywhere nearly so clearly.

To me, the two methods feel completely different; working psychically, the frequency changes and becomes much slower and heavier than in mediumship; going into a person's psyche makes me feel tired and drained of energy, whereas mediumship is uplifting and I feel full of energy.

It is not enough just to see images and describe them to the person. Once I've tuned in to his unconscious mind and blended with the images, I then have to actively work with those images, following them deeper, identifying other images within his unconscious mind that can help him, finding tools for him to work with to overcome his difficulties, and showing him how he can work with those images himself to bring about emotional healing and change.

Working with the unconscious mind can unlock many fears and doubts and insecurities. One lady rang me to say, 'I want to thank you for what you did for my daughter, it's totally changed her life.' I'd been working purely with her own unconscious symbols, which I'd explained during the sitting.

Other mediums might believe that the unconscious mind exists, but they don't like to think they're working with it. They only want the spirit world. But the point is that you can't be sure it's the spirit world if you don't know about all the different levels of consciousness that exist within us all.

I met a lady who said that a medium had told her that her son would die in a mountain accident, which had understandably upset her enormously. In fact all the medium was doing was reading the fears that existed within the woman's unconscious mind. Her son did mountain climbing and she used to worry about his safety; the possibility of his having a fatal accident was clearly in her mind. But the terrible thing is that many mediums will say things like this and then say that it's all come from the spirit world, which is both dangerous and dishonest.

When working psychically you can literally read someone's mind. But you can also go deeper into their mind and come to that part of their being that contains symbolic knowledge that has not been processed into everyday language. To interpret such symbols literally would completely miss their true significance and meaning.

Signs are something that we all understand. A sign represents something using a picture rather than words; looking at it, we know what it stands for. For instance road signs come in pictorial form but they have a fixed meaning that we have all learned, and so we understand them. If I said to an English person, 'What is a black dancing horse on a green background?' he would immediately recognise Lloyd's Bank. A flying dove with an olive branch in its mouth we know represents peace, and a crucifix represents the Church. Each of these signs is a symbol that has come to be associated with a particular meaning; seeing it, we immediately know what it means.

Seeing a symbol within a person's unconscious mind, we cannot attach a predetermined meaning to it in the same way at all. The symbolic language of the soul that you meet on travelling through these different levels of consciousness is entirely individual to the person you're working with. The only way to find out what these symbols are saying is to blend with them and feel the energy that is attached to them.

Actually, it's not the only way; the other way is to ask the person himself what his own symbols mean to him. This is different to working psychically. It's a dreamwork technique in which the person himself has to do the work because, clearly, he may not have any conscious idea what they mean.

In mediumship, using clairsentience, I blend with the person in spirit and can feel his energies, his emotions, his thoughts and memories. The very same process can be used in working with the unconscious mind. Within a person's mind, I see an image, or a symbol, or a particular part of his personality. I blend with this energy, and can feel the emotions, thoughts or memories associated with it.

The unconscious mind speaks mainly in pictures and symbols rather than words. These symbols can also take on human form so that you may see a medieval knight or a Native American or an old crone. These are aspects of that person's personality. When you blend with these, you can recognise parts of the personality that may have too much power or have been neglected.

The one trait that showed many times and in many forms was the perfectionist that most people have within them. The Perfectionist always finds fault and is never happy with anything that we have done, or anything that anyone else has done. When it has too much power over us, we become highly critical of ourselves and others. I know this is an aspect of my own personality that I have had to deal with. It's not easy. But, thank goodness, I believe I have conquered it now.

When I blend with a particular energy or see it personified as a particular character, I can identify the character traits that are causing trouble for that person. I use a very simple method when working with these personalities. I ask the person to think of a character from a film, soap or book, someone whose characteristics he can describe and identify with. Then every time the troubling feelings or thoughts start to arise, he has a name for them. He can identify those feelings with that fictional character so that whenever that character appears, he can do something to counteract it, such as creating a picture in his mind of closing a door on that character. This helps to reduce the power that the trait has over him so that he can come more into balance.

If I can use the analogy of a piano keyboard, how beautifully it plays, we think of this as life in perfect harmony; however, if one of the keys starts to stick, it throws out the whole song. Similarly, our Perfectionist is just one part of us. But if it's always criticising and telling us we're making mistakes, saying we're not good enough or not doing well enough, then the joy of life is taken away. If we can unstick that one key, or decrease the power of that one voice over us (so that one aspect does not have control over us), we can bring the whole back into balance. Otherwise the music, our life, is not melodic.

For many of us, one aspect of our being has too much power. But we either don't see that or don't want to admit it. Travelling into someone's mind, I would frequently see an archetypal picture of a cave or a fortress, and it wasn't always possible to enter. There would often be a dragon protecting the entrance to the cave, or the drawbridge would be up. Sometimes I would have to fight, or I might find something that would appease the protector of these realms so that it would trust me and let me in.

For many of us, there is also a part that is too weak. I would often see this part as a figure chained to a wall, or cowering in a corner of the dungeons in the castle. I would blend with this unconscious part of the person and talk to it in my mind. The psyche of the person I was working with would usually show me the way to it. It would also show the way to freedom, so I would be able to help it to escape from its dungeon.

The way out could be a simple mind exercise of climbing through the window and feeling the fresh grass outside. There could be a knight in shining armour who can rescue this lost being and give it the strength and the power and the nourishment that it needs.

The wonderful thing is that the psyche of each person already knows what s/he needs to do. I'm just helping the person to *access* that subconscious knowledge. But even this takes a great deal of work, finding mental images and bringing those mental images to the outer world.

One of the most common lost aspects of Self that I came across was the Inner Warrior, or inner strength. It would often be depicted in archetypal energy of warriors of different nations. Their power was not a warring power, but their strength of character and self-belief. Once we'd found the image of their inner strength, the exercise would be very simple. While showering, a person would imagine seeing them, and literally step into their skin – to feel them, and blend with them, and over time to become aware of different aspects of that character.

The inner warrior might be carrying a bracelet or a weapon, or the person might find something in the outer world that symbolised this part of themselves, a stick or amulet. By holding this in times of doubt or when feeling lost, s/he could bring up the energy and feel the power of that inner strength returning.

I hadn't heard of this method of working until I learned it from a shaman in the spirit world. Over a period of months, he helped me to use it, and I found myself doing these exercises and feeling my own courage rising, my own strength returning. I practised it, working on myself, for ten to twelve years before I started working in this way with other people.

The shaman told me that the shamans of old acknowledged and understood the qualities of the animals and the power within the natural world, so that when they needed those qualities within themselves they would wear the fur of the buffalo or the wolf. Those symbols are understood by the unconscious mind, and when we start to become aware of that level of our consciousness, we can access our own instinctive knowledge and power.

Often, when we have problems or doubts, the pictures from the unconscious come to our conscious mind and assist us through those problems. If we took the trouble and time to look at the symbols from the unconscious, we wouldn't have many of the problems that we do, because the answers lie within our very being, symbolically within our own psyche. We need to try and contact that symbolic world either through dreams or through meditation so we are constantly in touch with it and not just relying on it in times of crisis or trauma.

A few years back, a letter arrived saying I needed to go to the hospital for tests. I was terrified and broke out in a hot sweat, but in that instant I saw a picture in my mind of bottles breaking open and champagne being poured. 'Celebrate,' it was saying, 'it's not cancer.' My unconscious mind knew that I was going to be ok.

Whilst waiting for the results of all the tests, I can remember watching TV. A commercial break came and Dave got up to make coffee. At that moment I got into a real panic: in my mind I saw a fence falling down, and men with black capes coming towards me, riding black horses and circling all round me. Although scared, I was so fascinated by what was happening that I watched it. Just in time I pulled the fence up in front of me to stop them getting to me. So although I hadn't been overly anxious during those few weeks, there were occasions when that fear deep within me would be projected into images.

Some mediums work quite superficially and don't ever realise that, with the ability they have, they can go much deeper into a person's psyche and give real assistance. Most psychics I've known are quite happy to take on the role of fortune-teller. But I feel that if I just tell people what's going to happen, I'm taking their power away. I feel it's much better to empower them by giving them the tools they can use to bring about changes in their life.

One woman who is suffering from a neurological illness was told by a medium that it was because she had been a torturer in a past life. How is that empowering? That statement could have simply come from that medium's own belief system. Perhaps she believes in karma, or maybe she just saw a torturer projected from the woman's unconscious mind and attributed it to a past life, rather than blending with the image and finding that she's dealing with an aspect of the person that needs to be explored further. Either way, the medium has done nothing to help her client, and probably has little awareness that she is merely projecting her own beliefs onto other people, and attributing a person's unconscious images to the spirit world.

If a psychic hasn't done work on himself, a lot of the time he will be merely projecting his own emotions onto other people, or getting insights that are actually his own, and giving them out as if they're relevant to other people.

It's not just psychics, though, who don't want to work on themselves.

Many of us find it very difficult to express and take responsibility for our own feelings. Not showing emotion is a hangover from the Victorian era in which people never showed how they felt. Unfortunately many of us have inherited this trait from our parents' and grandparents' generations. Many people pass to the other side and feel great regrets that during life they hadn't been able to share their feelings.

Communication of emotion on all levels is so important. But we're not very good at it, so we tend to always be judging things just from our own point of view, rather than seeing how other people might be feeling.

Pride causes many problems, and we have such resistance to really saying how we feel, yet communication can solve so many of our emotional problems. If we could start at that level at the beginning of a relationship and really talk about things that are bothering us, then anger and hurt would not get stored up as it so often does.

Many of our messages to ourselves that come from our unconscious minds in the form of dreams or images, are telling us about our own emotions. They are a symbolic representation of our feelings about something that we have experienced. When we go into the image and work with it, we can change it. Our unconscious mind is constantly trying to get us to pay attention to the things inside ourselves that need to be heard. It may do this by repeatedly throwing up the same image; we might dream the same dream over and over, or have a series of dreams that seem to follow on one to the next. Or, if we don't take any notice of those dream images, they may get stronger and more insistent, or may turn into nightmares, so that finally we are forced to listen to them and work out what they are trying to tell us. The unconscious mind is amazingly creative in its attempts to make us take our own emotions and experiences seriously.

Sometimes when I was working, an image would come to my mind and I would know that it was mine and was not coming from the mind of the person with whom I was working. At other times, I would see an image that was not mine but, going into it, I'd know what it felt like. I could recognise the particular feelings held within it.

For instance, working with someone, I might see a man dressed in blue. When I blend with him, I see that he's frightened, and is trying to say something but is having difficulty getting the words out. His throat is blocked, and the frustration and anger of not being able to express his feelings have built up until he is completely unable to speak. Telling the person this, she might be able to relate to that difficulty in expressing emotions.

Now, when I blend further with him, I get a feeling of being very insecure. In my own life I have had that feeling, but the image projected from my own unconscious mind would be different. For me the feeling of insecurity would not be projected as a man in blue, whereas for this woman, insecurity was represented at this time by a man in blue who is unable to speak.

So, when I first see an image in my mind, I go into it and feel what it's saying. I am trying to sense the feelings that go with the image. Because whatever images we use, there are feelings underneath that need to be expressed or heard or released. Everyone's images would be different, but the range of feelings that each of us experiences is the same. Working in this way, the aim is to enter into the energy of an image, identify the feelings within it, and find some way that those feelings can be transformed.

The man in blue feels very insecure and he is afraid of rejection. I recognise that feeling of being afraid of rejection, I know it from within myself so I know what it feels like. I have spent a lot of time working with my own feelings, so I can usually quickly identify someone else's feelings when I blend with them. Without clairsentience it would be more difficult, because when you're clairsentient you can feel the energy of the different symbols, and go into them more, and that's the way I've worked with myself.

This is important, because many people need help with identifying their feelings. We spend so much time and effort trying to deny that we feel bad at all, that it can be very difficult to realise that we are actually feeling angry or jealous, or ashamed. We live in a world where people are constantly trying to make out that they don't have feelings, let alone problems. In response to the most horrendous experiences, people say, 'I'm fine,' 'It doesn't worry me,' and I listen to them and think, 'Well, I wouldn't be.' They are constantly trying to keep up the appearance of being ok, and in the process minimising the importance of their own emotional reactions and experiences, and of their own pain.

How often do people say, 'I'm really resentful,' or 'I've got a big problem with negativity.' Yet unless we acknowledge that something is troubling us or hurting us, we're not likely to be able to do anything about it.

Working with images, we can identify the feelings and also then work on the image to change it in some way. As it is a symbolic representation of a feeling, then working symbolically with it can release the emotions and shift the energy state associated with it. Mind exercises using visualisation can be a very effective way of bringing about change.

If we feel angry or upset at someone, for example a parent or partner or boss, then when we work within our own mind with the frustration or negativity that we feel, that person may sense when our energy has shifted, even though we haven't said anything to him. Sometimes we worry that we will have to change the way we act towards the other person in order to make anything shift, but the most important thing is working on ourselves, to free ourselves from the rage or pain that we feel. And it's amazing how often the other person changes in their attitude as a result of the work we have done on an ethereal plane.

Working psychically, you can contact the person's own higher self, which knows exactly what s/he needs to do to overcome a certain problem. You can work with dreams in the same way, blending with the dream image to sense the feelings associated with it, and you can glean so much information from that one symbol. I would find that a personal image often has more power than an archetypal image, because it's the person's own unconscious solution to their particular problem.

Most psychics don't give people mind exercises to work with. But I think it's up to the individual to do his or her own work to get the desired outcome. Working psychically should not be fortune telling, but helping a person to understand his or her own energies better, and to see what possibility or potential may come if s/he works with the images from the unconscious mind.

Above all, working psychically, I've learned that you can't assume anything.

Mediumistic Work

Working mediumistically, our mind travels through the mind of the person in spirit who we're working with. We pull out the information that is already in that person's mind, and how they're feeling emotionally. The medium's mind is constantly going backwards and forwards into the mind of the person in the spirit world.

It's a truism that like attracts like, and this applies as much when you're working with spirit as it does for any relationships that you have here on earth.

A spirit will communicate with a medium that he or she trusts, feels comfortable with, and shares some sort of affinity.

From the medium's point of view, the medium's mind will probably travel to whatever he or she is most interested in. So you can have three mediums working with the same person in spirit, and they'll bring out different aspects of that person.

For example, I used to work a lot with Simon James, an excellent young medium who would often contact young people. They would talk about music and tell him their favourite groups and songs. He'd also studied geography, so was very good at describing where they had lived. His hand would be moving, showing the shape of the place, and he could often get the actual town names.

Another medium was a businessman, and his mind would go into savings and investments and financial transactions.

On the other hand, I'm interested in houses and interior design and how things are made, so I would be giving details of how their house was decorated. I'd also say what perfume or make-up they wore, the pubs and drinks the men liked, their hat size, and other small, seemingly insignificant details that build up a picture of the person in spirit. I'd also find people's pets quite easily because I love animals. It was always lovely to know that a person's cat or budgie, or even a horse on one occasion, was still with them.

One of the myths of the Spiritualist Church was that if one medium tuned into another medium's contact, it would break the link. But I've done demonstrations with two other mediums, all working with the same contact, and I found that each medium would either be able to extend what the others were saying, or go into a completely different part of that person's life, and the information that came out could be very impressive.

Mediumship is an interactive process. You're interacting not just with the person in spirit, but also with the people in the audience, and sometimes it's the people on earth who are making the whole process more difficult than it needs to be. Mediumship works best if everyone involved is relaxed. But it can be hard to relax, as a medium, if people are not willing to participate.

In a demonstration in Telford Church, which was a lovely church to work in, I had a contact with a man who used to live in Aston, one of the poorer areas of Birmingham. He'd moved to Telford many years before and didn't live in modern housing. He said that his privy was at the bottom of the garden. He gave his name and all the names of the people who'd lived on the street, and he mentioned that he'd died on the privy.

I told this to a woman who denied it all, but the man was so insistent that he made me go back to her. I repeated the details and she finally said, 'Oh yes, I accept all that. I just don't know whether he died on the toilet!'

In Walsall, I once gave a description of a lady in spirit, including her name. She was talking to her daughter who was in the congregation. The daughter looked at me in horror and said, 'But how can she be talking to me? She's dead.'

I said, 'There's no such thing as death,' and she got up and walked out.

One evening, I was working in an independent church in Redditch in Worcestershire. The whole evening was fraught with the negativity of the people there. It really was like pulling teeth to get any answers from them at all.

One of the contacts gave his first name, surname, the manner of passing, yet no one in the congregation would accept a thing. I related various other details, but by this time I was fed up and could feel myself getting ready to walk off. Nobody accepted him so I said to the chairperson, 'I'm going to close the meeting. This is an insult to the spirit world.' Whereupon a woman said, 'Oh, I know the contact you had.'

I said, 'Well why didn't you speak up?' and she said, 'I was waiting for his middle name.' I don't think she thought for a moment about how the person in spirit felt.

A couple of other people then said, 'Yes, I recognised someone, but I didn't want to say I knew them in case you said too much.'

I later heard that a couple of women who had been working there around that time had been saying that a medium had to give the full name and address of every contact, otherwise people shouldn't listen. The people in the audience were therefore expecting something that can't always be fulfilled. Also, by their non-involvement, by not saying anything that might help with the contact, they were making it as difficult as possible for the medium!

Mediumship is hard enough as it is. When you're honestly trying to work, you can do without any added problems. The funny thing was that I knew from experience that the two women who'd been putting those ideas into people's minds weren't able themselves to give all the details of name and address. One of them once said, 'I've just had sex with my spirit guide,' so I hate to think what might have come next.

Guidelines are fine, but I've always been against rules – and against people setting themselves up as experts. For me, everything has to pass the test of plain common sense. Anything taken too literally can become ludicrous. As with the Spiritualist Church's dictate: 'Don't feed the medium anything.'

I know one medium who went to work down South. When he got there he was given a cup of tea. The rest of the family had an evening meal but he was excluded. He thought maybe he'd arrived too late, or they'd not understood he'd been travelling a long time and hadn't eaten. Either way, he went to bed hungry. In the morning he wasn't given any breakfast either. When he complained, saying he'd like something to eat, the woman, a committee member, said, 'Oh, I've always been told not to feed the mediums.'

Working in a local church, a lady communicated to me from the spirit world. Her daughter, quite an elderly lady herself, was in the Spiritualist Church for the first time, so had obviously not been indoctrinated with the Church's idea of not helping the medium.

I started describing her mother in spirit, and she leaped out of her chair shouting, 'That's my mum!' She was so excited, and her mum was overjoyed at being met in such a way. It was wonderful to see, and it made the whole communication much easier. When you're working, doubts always pop into your mind and you wonder, 'Have I got that right?' and that can interfere with your mediumship. People sometimes don't think about how those in the spirit world feel about their reactions.

In Canada, I found that people were very excited when they experienced a contact with the spirit world. Communication from a loved one was quite rare, because the mediums there don't give evidence of life after death. I was working once in Vancouver, British Columbia, and I had a contact for an elderly man. He was absolutely amazed and so happy. He'd been going to the Spiritualist Church for years and they'd never given spirit contacts. They tended to talk in generalisations or give information about the colours of the aura such as, 'I can see a lot of orange round you, so you're going to come into some money soon.' What's that about? I'm still waiting to come into the money.

They would say that what they were doing was mediumship, but to me the whole purpose of mediumship is to prove life after death. Of course, for some people that's still not enough, they want their fortunes told or the spirit world to get them out of trouble. It's incredible how many people still expect their parents in the spirit world to sort out their problems for them. This to me is not what mediumship is for; each of us has to learn to be self-reliant and not look to anyone else, whether a parent or a medium or a spirit, to solve our problems, because in the end any decisions we make have to be our own.

CHAPTER TEN

Training Mediums:
Questions and Answers

What did you teach in your workshops?

I taught mediumship and psychic awareness, but self-development
and dream workshops became my speciality. The main goal was to
help people become more aware of themselves. You have to recognise the Self in order to develop its potential. But of course most of
us resist finding out about ourselves, at least at first.

The workshops helped people to recognise who and what they
were. People would feel the closeness of the spirit world and the reality
of their own spirit, which empowered them, and the workshops often
led to personal breakthroughs. I could see big changes in people over
time, which was very rewarding.

The dream workshops in particular were a great joy for me. Dreams
contain powerful messages from our unconscious mind. If we take
the time to listen to our dream-maker, we become more in contact
with our emotions. We connect with our own intuitive wisdom
through the language of our own soul. Dreams can tell us how we feel,
what we need to do, and they can warn us of things that are threat-

ening us. Many great leaders of our time have had inspiration while in a dream state.

In the spiritualist world, there is a general belief that spirit talks to us in dreams. Although this can happen, I tend to think that, in the main, it is different parts of our own being which guide us through our dreams. I also believe that we are the only ones who can interpret our own dreams. Although others can help along the way, no one else can tell us what they mean.

In one dream workshop, a couple from Holland had come with their seventeen-year-old daughter. The girl had always been locked into her emotions and a little distant from her parents. She'd had a particularly powerful dream and it took a lot of time, one to one, to work with it. But at the end of the week she was a different person. She was laughing, carefree, playing with the cat at the College, and so much happier. Her parents were so glad to see the difference. All credit to her for working with the dream. It's not always easy to face up to what's really going on inside us.

I found that people in Australia and Europe were far more open to this sort of work than those in the UK, whose view tended to be, 'Just get on with your life. What good does it do talking about dreams?' Fortunately, that attitude is changing. People are actively questioning their roles in this life and doing more to overcome their psychological problems.

Dreams are not the only way of accessing the unconscious mind. We can enter a different level of consciousness using meditation; then, journeying into the self, we can interpret the visions or images that appear at that level of consciousness. The transpersonal approach can be used without dreams, simply by travelling into the mind, drawing what we see, in paint or crayons, and then interpreting those images. Insights can be gained from the pictures by exploring why particular colours were used, and going deeper into the symbols to find out what they represent. Splitting into groups of three, we would work with the images that had been produced within the meditation.

Sometimes students would jump up and dance and sing and be happy; great breakthroughs were made, and their lives would become easier and more joyful. We can't underestimate the power it gives us to know who we are and where we're coming from.

Often we become the victim in one way or another. It's only when we stop and ask ourselves why we keep getting into the same predicaments, without learning, that we can break that cycle. Often, people go from one abusive relationship to another and blame each partner when things go wrong. We have to recognise that these attractions occur at a level we may not even be aware of. We project our fears of rejection or abandonment or whatever. We project the image of self as victim, which an abusive person will be attracted to on a purely unconscious level.

It's not easy to shed those heavy boots of misery or despair. Yet if we look at ourselves and work on ourselves, we find that, just like Cinderella, we too have wonderful glass slippers that we can dance with.

In the psychic workshops I tried to awaken peoples' awareness of their own sixth sense, which we all have, and which is as natural as seeing, hearing, tasting, touching and smelling. Many people think that psychic ability is merely for telling fortunes but, once we'd awakened that sixth sense, they realised how much it could tell them about themselves.

If we're wise, we listen to our sixth sense, or gut instinct. Unfortunately, in the past, I wasn't always wise enough to listen to mine, but, when we do use it, it can be a wonderful instrument for self-help, and it's quite amazing what we're able to sense.

One of my students, Maureen, came to a lot of my groups. She had a short fuse, and for weeks we simply did an exercise that looked at colour. A colour card was placed in an envelope and each person had to hold the envelope and say what colour s/he felt it was. Maureen became so good at it she could instantly tell us what colour was inside. If she had red, which often signifies anger, she would throw the envelope across the room, and cry out, 'Don't give me red, don't give me red!'

In the psychic workshops we used to work with colour, music, meditation and various exercises to make people more aware of their auric field. One of the techniques to show that we have an effect on the atmosphere around us was to have people sitting in a circle and, after talking to them for a while, I'd send someone out. I would take a chair that someone in the room had been sitting on and place it in front of me. The person outside would then come back in and sit on the chair and tell us all about the person who'd previously sat on it. It was amazing how much they could say about that person's personality, feelings and mood state.

If you think of a normal day, how many times might this happen to you? You set out feeling fine, you go to work on the tube or bus, then when you get off you find you're not feeling as good. It's possible that you're feeling the energy from the person who's been sitting on the seat before you.

Which is another good reason to recognise our need to work on ourselves. The negativity within all of us is spread to others, not just through what we say and do, but also through our thoughts, our energy field and our emotional state. We are all linked, connected and affecting others whether we're conscious of it or not, and many of us are responsible for spreading negativity by not working on ourselves at a deep level.

After a few days the students would be so tuned in to their psychic ability that I could send someone out the room, touch someone in the group lightly on the shoulder, then get the person back in and say, 'Tell me all about the person I've just touched,' and they would do so in great detail.

Our psychic abilities can help us make choices, prevent us from making bad decisions, and give warnings of problems occurring.

Many years ago, I was due to travel to London for some transpersonal training.

I was merely thinking about the journey when I suddenly got a real thump. I had a gut feeling that I shouldn't go by car as usual, so I went by train. I learned later that there'd been a multiple pile-up on the M1 at just the time I would have been making my journey.

The sixth sense is a very powerful tool. The indigenous people of many continents accept this despite superstition and religion often condemning it. Using their sixth sense, they know where to find water, where there is safe ground, or when there's going to be a storm. The more civilised we become, and the more clothes we wear, the less in touch we are with this wonderful ability that we all have.

Whilst the sixth sense can be used to help other people, the main benefit as I see it is to help ourselves. If we all learned how to listen to this almost magical quality that exists within us, we would be much less dependent on others to help us out. And we would be far more accepting of ourselves.

In a dream workshop, there was an elderly woman who was always very pleasant, but a sober character and always very uptight. We were working in pairs with dreams at the time: each person would tell a dream to their partner who would then work with the ideas and images in the dream. The elderly woman had a dream about a cold fish. Her partner couldn't get anywhere with the dream, so put her hand up for help. I went over and asked the elderly woman what the cold fish reminded her of, and she shouted out 'Sex!'

Towards the end of the week we always had a dance in the bar, so I asked her if she was coming and she said, 'Oh no, I've never danced in my life.' I persuaded her to come, and she spent the night smiling and laughing and dancing all night and enjoyed herself immensely. Obviously something had shifted for her.

It's amazing what we can get from simple things in our dreams when we take the time to journey into them.

Can anyone be a medium?

I used to believe that anyone could be a medium, but now I honestly don't think that's the case. It's certainly possible within a workshop to make some people aware of the spirit world, so that they can sense it or see it, and that can bring a lot of joy into their lives. But not everyone is capable of being truly mediumistic. Similarly, we can all learn to paint or make music but, other than amusing our families or driving them to distraction with the racket we're making, very few attempts will result in being able to paint like Monet or write music like Vivaldi.

I don't think mediumship should be taken on board lightly. Many people go to Spiritualist Churches because they've lost a loved one. In some churches, within a very short time those people will be sitting in a circle for mediumship. They suddenly start thinking, 'I could do this,' when what they really need is to grieve fully.

When people sit in such circles, a lot of power games and bruised egos come into play. Because many of those people are not actually mediumistic, and have not been accepted as healers, they are apt to feel they can't do *anything*. This not only has the effect of discouraging them from being themselves, but may also hinder them in finding out what they truly are able to do. Many real mediums – including myself – have suffered in these groups as a result. I remember many years ago a committee member at Sutton Coldfield Church telling me he would hold me back by my shirt-tail – presumably because his own efforts at mediumship hadn't been that rewarding.

Anyone who has not worked on their own emotional problems will simply project their own fears, hopes and unresolved issues onto the person they're talking to. This is true whatever career a person follows, but it is of particular consequence if that person's chosen field is one in which they are purporting to help others.

Although false messages may bring some comfort to people in the short term, it's just not honest. Absolute proof of life after death takes a bit more than just saying, 'I've got your mother here.' Receiving a true contact from the spirit world can have a profound effect on people and their view of life.

I have been accused in my lifetime of saying many things that I didn't say, and I've been able to rectify them. If my dad, who's in the spirit world, was reported as saying something that he didn't actually say, he wouldn't easily be able to rectify it. Knowing my dad, that would upset him greatly – as I'm sure it would most people.

A medium has to develop his or her mediumistic ability, but also has to take responsibility for everything that s/he does with mediumship. As mediums, we must make absolutely sure that we are making contact with people's loved ones. We need to know we're with the spirit world, that we're getting the message right, and that we're not leaving people's loved ones in a state of frustration, anger or despair after contacting them.

How can mediums be helped to develop their mediumship?

Developing mediumship takes a lot of hard work. After a demonstration I would always go back over it to see where I went wrong, where I could have got more information out, or where I'd slipped from the mediumship into the psyche.

To give accurate and detailed information you need not just the name, which you sometimes don't get, but also a description of that person, their personal characteristics, for example that she loved stockings, wore high heels, what makeup she used to use, how she did her hair, what colour she painted her nails. Or an older person would be able to bring back memories of his past, in which case you can tease out details that are relevant and convincing to the person listening. The medium has to have the dedication to do it all themself, to push themself, to get more details, and to go further than just general information.

There is a huge expectation when working on the platform – people want specific information that they can relate to. If you give too many details that they have to go and check, the energy of the moment is lost, and they think it's rubbish. The group energy gets the whole thing going; sometimes the energy feels flat, and you have to know how to lift it. So it's very stressful. You have to have confidence, be good at thinking on your feet, and get lots of practice. It helps a great deal to observe people who have years of experience. You have to be willing to keep learning and changing. In platform work, probably the most important thing is that you're relaxed. You have to be yourself. It won't work if you're anxious or under-confident.

Every medium works individually, so the problem with teaching mediumship is that if we stick to the so-called rules and say, 'This is how you're supposed to work,' then we won't help students to find the way that works best for them. Everyone does it differently, and that's fine, as long as you keep an open mind.

When I was about to demonstrate I would always listen to a tape of Tina Turner before I went in to the church to get my energy up. Some of my colleagues thought it was a little odd, but then I am odd.

Our chakras resonate to sound, so upbeat music can lift our energy. During a demonstration you have to expend a lot of energy to contact and interact with the spirit world. It's not just sitting back to let them talk. Mediumship is an active, not a passive, process so it's essential to raise the energy within yourself.

Other people would sit quietly and meditate while listening to relaxing music, but this didn't work for me. Many people think that in order to connect to spirit you need peace and quiet, but mediumship is a very personal thing and there is no one way that is right for everyone.

For me, the quiet time when I would sit and commune with my helpers in the spirit world would always take place prior to the journey to the group or demonstration. Dave would always say an hour or so before, 'I won't bother talking, you're not here now.' I was already on a different level of consciousness by the time I was in the shower and getting ready to go. I would put on my medium's clothes and it was as if symbolically I recognised that these were my working clothes. I would do the same in private sittings and then, as soon as I'd finished work, I'd change back into jeans and a T-shirt, feet on the ground and back to this life again.

It's always essential to be confident when demonstrating. This is quite difficult in the beginning because you don't know what depth or quality you're going to be able to achieve; in fact you don't really have a clue whether it's going to work at all.

Many years ago I met an excellent medium from South Wales called Dell Round, who was the leader of the Swansea Psychic Centre. Public work was fairly new to me then, and one of the exercises she taught me was to stand in front of a mirror and blow my own trumpet, saying, 'God, they're lucky to have me tonight!' She stayed at our home once, before a public demonstration. She was so nervous I took her by the shoulders, pointed her at the mirror and reminded her to do it herself, and she was fine. After that, I used that technique with many students and it worked wonderfully.

To help anyone else with their mediumship, you have to be honest about your own; how you're working, and what you're sensing and experiencing. When teaching psychic awareness or mediumship, people look to you for guidance; working with subtle and fleeting feelings and sensations, they need you to provide them with a reliable reality-check.

When I was working with the spirit world, giving a person in the audience details of a contact, I would sometimes realise that I'd left the spirit world and had gone into the psyche of the person sitting in front of me. Then I would always say, 'I'm not getting this from the spirit world now, I'm getting it from you.' However, several mediums I worked with told me, 'You shouldn't say that to people.'

The mind is so powerful that all of us can project images that are so strong that clairvoyants and mediums can actually see them. If they don't have an understanding of the subconscious mind, although the energy and the vibration are different, they will think it comes from the spirit world. From my experience of training mediums, there is great reluctance to being told they're working psychically. They just want spirit, but if you haven't travelled to the depths of the psyche how do you know the difference?

Some mediums are actually a lot better psychically than they are mediumistically, and they would be using a lot of information gained psychically. But the first criterion for me in mediumship is honesty. I wouldn't want someone to think I was getting something from spirit that I was actually taking straight out of their own mind.

It's also important to be honest about your own feelings. I remember another time when I was working with Simon, the medium I mentioned before, in Gateshead, County Durham. We got on well personally as well as mediumistically, and we shared many similar ideas. He was a young man at the time, around thirty. One contact he was doing was absolutely brilliant, his mediumship was really amazing, but suddenly I felt something within me that I didn't like. When I questioned myself, I realised that I was actually envious. Driving back home, I told him about it but he couldn't understand it at all. He said how well my demonstration had gone, and that there was no need for me to feel such envy. But I had felt envious, and it was important for me to acknowledge it.

At times, we probably all feel envious of someone. There will be times when we wish that our contacts had gone that well, just as we all at times feel disappointment or anger or resentment. These emotions are part of being human. But if we don't acknowledge them or express them, then I believe the envy or anger or whatever will grow within us. It's important to recognise the negative qualities within ourselves.

Ideally, when we're learning we should be able to express our fears and doubts and insecurities to those who are purporting to help us. A teacher, by being honest about his or her own feelings and experiences, gives his students encouragement to do the same.

I remember in the early days doing workshops in Spain, San Lo would draw so close that I was always heavily overshadowed by her. She's a bit of a tinker and has a good sense of humour. Once, she said through me, though I don't remember saying it, 'We're now going to have some fun.' She walked around the group and everyone felt really warm. She stopped, turned, clapped her hands and walked back the other way, and everyone suddenly went really cold.

Years later, I told this to a very well-known medium. The following day, while giving a public trance demonstration at the College, she went into a so-called trance and told everyone that she was going to change the temperature of the room. She then asked the people there if they felt it. I was perfectly conscious all the time and could tell that no one felt a thing. A couple of people at the front put their hands up and other hands slowly appeared, even though nothing had happened at all! Clearly a case of the Emperor's new clothes.

Sadly, there are plenty of mediums, often highly revered by their students, who set themselves up as being infallible, are less than honest, and even feel the need to cheat.

CHAPTER ELEVEN

Guides and Helpers:
Questions and Answers

Chapter Outline

Do we all have a guardian angel?

Do you have a spirit guide?

What is channelling?

What is meant by higher realms of consciousness? Can you connect with these?

Have there been times when you have been frightened?

What is psychic attack?

Exercising the power of your mind

Do we all have a guardian angel?

We can all get help from the spirit world. A guardian angel is the modern description of the old Victorian guides and helpers, who usually seemed to appear as a Native American, a Chinese, or a nun. I have always had great difficulty with that. I believe that what's actually happening is that people are personifying an archetypal energy in terms defined by their own mind-set.

If they sense an energy that is gentle, strong, spiritual and has a quiet authority, they might say, yes, definitely it's a nun. Most of us have a fairly fixed idea of what we think certain people are: that's the basis of stereotypes. So, if we feel an energy helping us from the spirit world, we call it a guardian angel or spirit guide, and we're likely to personify that energy into an archetypal image. For example many people describe their spirit guides as priests, Egyptians, or Tibetan monks. All these represent similar characteristics and have similar energies.

Do you have a spirit guide?

I have a spirit guide, or helper, called San Lo. She told me that she was Chinese and used to work in the brothels where the English ships came in. In those days, everyone was smoking opium and the children in the brothels were used as prostitutes. She would look after those children and befriend them. I don't think she was a prostitute as such, but she would sometimes give herself to a man or woman if they were shunned by the others, perhaps because they were badly disfigured. She would give them the love that they wouldn't otherwise get.

She's a very joyful personality and adores children. She spends her time quite happily now, looking after the little children that have passed through starvation, that people have not cared about: tiny bundles of humanity that pass to the spirit world never having received love. San Lo helps those beautiful beings in the spirit world. She has always been very caring and compassionate. It was she who urged me to raise funds for Croatia.

She's also quite excitable. She loves men. At a demonstration she would always flirt with the youngest, best-looking guys. That's not me at all! Men used to fall in love with her. They'd really love her from their souls. She would go round every single person in the room and give them each something. She would then walk over to the best-looking guy in the room and say, 'You can walk me to my seat.'

San Lo had the ability to make people not just feel her, but also to feel the boundless love that she had for them. She made everything so easy, and always managed quite effortlessly to bring about wonderfully positive experiences for people.

If you are clairsentient, someone in the spirit world can draw so close into your auric field or your mind that, although you would still appear to be you, you are talking from their mind. I would be able to give a talk or do a workshop while completely under the influence of this mind in the spirit world. San Lo would draw close and we'd gradually blend together so that she would direct what was happening in the workshop. The workshops we did together were usually very successful – except that if anyone interrupted, I wouldn't know what I'd just been talking about!

Once, while doing such a workshop, I was so heavily overshadowed by San Lo that when it was over it felt as if my insides were vibrating at a different rate to the outside. It took me two days to come back to feeling together again.

This is one of the dangers of overshadowing: afterwards I'd be upset over the most trivial things. I'd play the prima donna or just act out of character for me.

San Lo would normally only appear if I was working with a group of people. She would usually have more profound insights than me, and would talk to people about their core issues and most deeply rooted problems, as she had insights into their very being.

I was working in Australia in a retreat in the bush. Each morning I'd get up early and sit with one of the students, Bessie, who became a dear friend. Although she'd lived in Australia for twenty years she still maintained her Lancashire accent. We'd sit there on the balcony listening to the dawn chorus while we smoked our cigarettes, quietly happy in each other's company.

Marilyn, a friend of Bessie, was an amazing woman; she had a natural ability to create laughter and humour and had a beautiful singing voice. One morning she came out and sat beside us. Bessie told me later that San Lo said something to her. It only took a minute and a half, and I have no memory of it at all. Bessie said, 'You did something for Marilyn that has released her from a burden that she's been carrying for forty years.'

San Lo has always had a wonderful ability to touch a person's soul and really get to the heart of a problem. A man was about to get married, and she was quite adamant that he shouldn't. He told me later that he'd seen another medium afterwards, who'd said that no one from the spirit world would say something like that. He married;

within six months the whole thing fell apart, and his wife later had to be committed to a mental hospital. He was a broken man.

What is channelling?

Channelling is actually far more complicated than most people realise. The first thing that happens when I'm channelling my spirit guide is a change of energy in the room, a coldness coming from the floor. It takes me a moment to calm my mind as the mind is like a butterfly, and the mind of a medium more so than most!

San Lo comes into my mind and helps to instill a sense of quiet, to put me into the right frame to communicate. Then she's here with me. I am in a state of trance and she speaks through me. Afterwards, I have little or no recollection of what has been said. When she has finished it takes me quite a time to reorientate to my surroundings and myself.

I often feel completely disorientated afterwards. I am tired because I am using my energy to aid the communication. That's why it can help if other people are present: their input adds energy. Mediums also use the energy of the people they're working with. After a demonstration, some people in the audience will be tired because their psychic energy has been drawn out of their auric field.

What is meant by higher realms of consciousness? Can you connect with these?

Each of us has our own vibration. We're all on a different frequency – it's not just personality, it's about this natural pulling together of the same frequency, an attunement between people. We can gel with some better than others.

When we don't get on with someone, sometimes it's simply that we're vibrating at a different frequency. The human tendency, of course, is to find fault with the other person, but that's not it: our auric field just vibrates at different rates, and different frequencies don't match.

Likewise, with mediumship, there may be difficulties when the communicator in spirit and the medium don't really gel. Then, others in the spirit world will be there to help adjust these frequencies so that we *can* communicate. Sometimes, the medium may say, 'It won't work, I can't blend with this person,' and spirit facilitates, so that the blending is easier. Even then, though, it doesn't always work.

The minds of the people in the spirit world act as a transformer. My vibration as a medium would be too heavy to tune in directly to a higher evolved energy, but I can do it through a guide, to tune in by degree.

San Lo has a similar outlook to mine on life and a similar attitude towards people. But she has more dedication. She is evolving in the spirit world and can reach upwards as well as downwards. She claims she's not highly evolved! She likes looking after children here, talking to people here, but, despite what she says of herself, she can also reach into a mind that's considerably more highly evolved, to bring ideas, healing, philosophy, help and information from those higher levels of consciousness.

While blending with a highly evolved mind in the spirit world, San Lo can blend with me and give me higher thoughts of what everything is about. In this way, energies can be transformed down. It would be impossible for most of us here to do that directly, without help, as our energy is much denser and the power would simply be too strong.

During a demonstration I would sometimes feel such a power from the spirit world. It was amazing. I would see a lilac-pink column of light beside me. Those colours didn't match my idea of that type of powerful energy. So initially I had problems linking the energy that I could see with the incredible power that I felt.

There are different levels of evolution. When I used to work with another of my spirit guides, Red Cloud, on philosophy, for instance, he would see things in a much clearer way than I could. He would put those ideas across through San Lo. Red Cloud would also be able to blend with a higher vibration so that messages would come from an even more highly evolved soul than his. So sometimes messages and philosophical thoughts would be coming from intelligences *far* higher than mine. And, at a guess, there might be somewhere between six and ten intermediaries involved.

Various mediums have connected with higher energies in this way to bring messages and understanding from highly evolved beings. It's a very delicate process, but, with humankind sending their consciousness out, and the spirit world sending theirs out too, many obstacles can be overcome.

Various well-known higher energies have been channelled but, whatever the source of the channelled information, the overall message was the same. It is only the belief systems that were different. A Christian medium would tune into one spirit source, a Buddhist medium would tune into another, but, because communication from higher minds still comes from different points-of-view, the words, the emphasis and the interpretation are all slightly different. Even in channelling higher energies, the pathways to the source go along different lines.

The many worlds that we can inhabit are far more numerous than most people recognise. Knowledge and understanding from much higher energies are delivered from different levels into the mind of another energy and yet another energy, and so on downwards.

Have there been times when you have been frightened?

When I started sitting in the first mediumship group, back in my early thirties, we were told by the leader and his wife that we shouldn't even sit and meditate on our own, let alone sit for mediumship, without the protection of the group leader. They said this so often that I came to fear what might happen if I did.

On one occasion, Roy, the brilliant medium I mentioned earlier, and his friend, Len, who was also mediumistic, came round to my house and we had a little group.

When they left, I sensed the presence of a man in the house. I was very frightened and, because I'd trusted the group leader and his wife, I really thought that I'd attracted something unpleasant from the spirit world. Years later, after questioning and studying the power of the mind, I realised that this was just a personified energy: it was simply a projection of my own fear.

Often, when people are afraid, they see a figure that seems very real, and they think that they're seeing a spirit, when in fact what they're seeing is the energy of that fear projected outwards from their own unconscious mind.

Years later, I was in London for one of the training sessions in transpersonal psychology. A friend and client had paid for me to stay in a really nice hotel. I'd been out at the workshop all day, had taken my meal in my room and gone for a bit of a walk. I was feeling tired. I went to bed but then woke up to find Dave was standing at the bottom of the bed.

It was so real. We spoke and he got into bed and put his arm round me. We were just starting to make love when I came to and realised it was all a figment of my imagination. He wasn't there at all!

My interpretation was that my own insecurity and my need to have him with me had brought it about. It had nothing to do with the spirit world. It shows, I think, how our deep desires can be made real and manifest purely through the power of the mind.

Once, I was driving to Sainsbury's in Mere Green near Sutton Coldfield. I stopped at traffic lights and looked down at my arm. I could see a skeleton of another arm sitting on top of mine. I was terrified. I phoned Ann Drury, a psychotherapist who I was friendly with, as I knew that she could deal with this type of experience. She said that she and her husband, Brian, would sit down that evening at ten o'clock to clear whatever negativity was around me.

At ten o'clock, I went upstairs and lay down on the bed quietly to see what would happen. I became aware of Brian's kind face in front of me. It was as if he was holding me. And then a horrible jellylike thing appeared, resting on my abdomen. Suddenly I saw a fire, which looked like a burning bracken bush, and the jelly-thing suddenly exploded into the air, shattering into a thousand pieces.

I phoned Anne and told her what I'd seen. She said that Brian had used the power of his mind to protect her, surrounding her in a circle of light, so that the negativity couldn't affect her. First of all, she had tried to smash the substance that she could see with a hammer, and then she set fire to it, and it shattered into the air into lots of pieces like little stars.

She was amazed that I had seen everything that happened. She later wrote a paper on it for the Runnings Park Centre in Malvern. She also described the woman she saw. It was someone I knew, someone involved in a local church, whose envy or jealousy had been directed at me. She obviously had quite a strong mind!

A lot of people have similar experiences. They become frightened, thinking they've stumbled into the spirit world. But this had nothing to do with spirit; it was something I was picking up psychically. At the time, my work with mediumship was becoming successful and there were a lot of green eyes in people who I had been working with.

San Lo told me, years ago, that she would protect me from any negative energies from the spirit world – if like attracts like, then hopefully I wouldn't attract too many negative spirits – but it was my responsibility to protect myself from the negative energies of people on earth. After that, whenever I went to bed at night, I would always use my mind to cover the house in a mist, making it invisible, to protect it from psychic attack from the minds of people here.

What is psychic attack?

If we wish ill on someone, if we go around cursing him or even wishing him dead, if we're constantly thinking about him in that way, then it will affect him; if he is sensitive, he will see it and feel it. We might be attacking someone psychically and not even realise it. We have constantly to be looking at ourselves, realising the power of our own negative thoughts.

We also have to be aware that when we are open and sensitive, we are also vulnerable. One of the reasons that my clairsentience was so strong was that I trusted people. I was very naïve. I assumed that everyone was honest, and I was quite happy to blend with anybody. I thought everyone was coming from the same place of wanting to help people and help the spirit world.

After I left the first group, they kept trying to get me to go back and I wouldn't. One day, I was walking along the road outside my house, and I felt this incredible anger and frustration. It hit me like a dart. In my mind I grabbed hold of it, because I knew it wasn't my own; I made a paper plane of it and simply threw it back, with the power of my mind, to whoever had sent it. I did this instinctively. I could see, in my mind, that it landed at the front door of the house where that group held its meetings.

People can send fear or hatred to someone else purely by the power of their mind, and in some form this will affect the person it is sent to. Even if the person doesn't see the form, they will be able to feel it. We can conjure up all sorts of feelings and send them to others. Some people even pay others to do it for them.

A few years back, a West Indian lady approached me via another medium. She was absolutely terrified, saying that little patches of fire had started to break out in her home, and her son's hair had been cut and left on his pillow while he was asleep. Many people would have dismissed her as mad! I sat down and sent my mind to the situation. I literally jumped out of the chair because I recognised that it was far too powerful for my mind to deal with. There was no way I was going to go in there.

A man in Leicestershire specialised in helping people who were under psychic attack, so I went to see him. He told me just to tell him what had happened, but not to mention any names or places because, believe it or not, some people's minds are so powerful that they could trace him simply through our conversation. It all sounded terribly weird. Anyway, I told him the story and left.

A couple of weeks later I went back to see him. He looked awful; his eyes were sunken and he'd lost a lot of weight. He told me it was one of the worst cases of voodoo that he had ever come across. He'd traced it back to one of the islands in the West Indies where blood sacrifices had been made, and he hoped he had dealt with it. He didn't make a charge; he just worked in this way to try to help people, but at what cost to his health?

I checked back to the West Indian lady and she said that the attacks had stopped. But I felt so bad about putting him through all that that I never asked him for help again.

This was an extreme example of psychic attack. People reading it may think that it's a load of rubbish, but many of us have suffered when other people's negativity has been directed at us. I think there will be many people reading this who have experienced less extreme examples of psychic attack, but may not have understood what was happening. Sadly, many such incidents are attributed to something evil from the spirit world.

Exercising the power of your mind

As a student, I was walking down the grand staircase at the College with a friend when I saw her husband at the bottom of the stairs. I told her and she was a bit miffed because she couldn't see him at all. When she got home, he said that that evening he'd been sitting sending out loving thoughts to her at the Hall. So those thoughts obviously arrived and my mediumistic capability had allowed me to see an image of the sender, although it wasn't anything to do with the spirit world.

While I was at home, just before travelling to Vancouver Island to work, I thought I'd like to talk to Brian Robertson, who was a medium and Reverend of the Inner Quest Foundation there. About ten minutes later he phoned me. As we were talking, I projected my mind to where he was and said, 'It's pretty cloudy over there.' He was surprised and confirmed that it was. I could see that he'd put his coffee down half finished and it was getting cold, so I suggested he drink the rest.

Whilst many people might think that someone in spirit was telling me these things about him, I can honestly say there was no spirit at work, it was just me using my mind.

The fact is that everyone has psychic ability to a greater or lesser degree. Most of the time, we are restricting and confining the working of our minds. Not only are we unaware of our psychic abilities, but also we are largely unaware of how our minds affect our reality.

Whether we are habitually thinking positively or negatively, our thoughts have incredible power.

If we send a prayer out to the universe, asking the angels to take care of something, and truly let it go, then the angels will take care of it. But we don't do this.

Instead, we get tension headaches and bad backs, and all the other ailments that stress brings us, because we find it so difficult to trust in the universe and to surrender control. We get bogged down so much in mundane worries and problems that we stop our minds from being free. For our minds to be free, we have to work through our problems and let them go. We have to become aware of who and what we really are. Because, at the end of the day, all things and all problems pass. We are simply spirit.

We are all human and when we're in a negative mind-set, it can be very difficult to get out of it. Sometimes we have to use the power of the mind to lock those thoughts away until we're ready to deal with them; otherwise that negativity or anger will be indiscriminately released onto everyone and everything we meet.

When something is really bothering me, I use the image of a big heavy bank vault door. I put the worries and negative thoughts inside and turn a big lock on the door. Then I can concentrate on the day and when I feel ready to face those worries, I go back and take them out again and work out what the problem really was. This sounds simple but it takes a lot of practice. I was in my late forties before I managed to do it effectively. We can use the mind to store away problems we can't deal with at that time.

When we allow ourselves to worry and worry, we can't think straight. We may become completely immobilised. So it's a good idea to have some way of switching your mind off to those worries about things that you cannot influence or do anything about. Many will resolve with time, and if they do not, then sooner or later we must go back to that place where we've stored them and start to sort them out.

Years ago, we moved house and we had two mortgages. I was worried about money and how we'd manage if something went wrong. I remember driving along and I couldn't seem to stop myself from worrying. Waves of panic kept flooding over me and I felt terrible.

Suddenly, from nowhere, I could see a fireplace in my mind. I started mentally decorating our new home and, after a while, I realised that I didn't feel stressed any more. Instinctively, my mind knew that all those negative thoughts were doing me no good and, to defend me against them, it had thrown up the image of the fireplace: it was a simple device to start me thinking about something positive.

Whatever we are worrying about, if we take our mind to something positive it can help, to a certain degree, to overcome the stress. But it takes a strong mind to do it. When we're in this negative, fearful state of mind, the mind works itself further and further down into depression and fear and negativity. This becomes self-perpetuating. We need to take the initiative so that we are in control of the mind. Otherwise it's like a wild horse, it goes in its own direction. And again it will affect us emotionally, physically and spiritually.

One simple visualisation exercise when we feel things are out of our control is to imagine catching that wild horse, taking it somewhere peaceful and letting it gradually calm itself. However you are feeling, if you can find some image that seems to represent your emotion at that moment, then you can work with that image in your mind, imagining changing it in some way. This helps you to release some of the worry and fear energy that has built up around it.

Simple exercises will help to break the stress cycle and the mind's journey into negativity, and start you feeling more positive. Everybody knows that worrying doesn't help anything. Many people would say, 'Oh, I can't help it,' but the fact is that we can do something about it. It just takes practice and effort to strengthen the mind.

Putting energy into a mental image is a powerful way of creating a different reality. Another useful exercise is to find a personal symbol that has power and energy for you, and to regularly imagine it surrounding you or standing next to you to protect you. What you are actually doing is strengthening the aura. For instance, you can use a power animal, which will make you feel stronger and more confident.

If we are low in self-confidence we are vulnerable to negativity or psychic attack. We also need to realise that like attracts like so, if we are constantly thinking negative thoughts about ourselves or others, we will also be opening ourselves to negativity from other people. If, for instance, business rivals or people trying to outdo us are sending us negative thoughts, we will be less able to resist these. Maybe this is one reason our ventures don't always succeed.

If we focus on thinking positive thoughts and learn to strengthen the auric field, then, at an unconscious level, other people will sense that we are strong and confident and their negativity will not penetrate so easily or cause us problems.

When I was working with the shaman in the spirit world, he gave me a snow wolf as a protector. In Egyptian mythology Anubis was the protector between the two worlds, so the idea of protectors is nothing new. The shaman told me that the wolf would appear whenever I needed it. We are affected by the negativity and fears of others around us; we can suddenly sense feelings coming from the people we are in contact with. So before I went out, I would visualise my wolf around me, and the image of the wolf would protect me from these energies.

A while after I started doing this, I met a friend who was a medium and a psychologist. As we were walking along, she said, 'Oh, you've got a wolf walking beside you.' Just thinking about this wolf made him real, to the extent that others could see him too.

Around the same time, I did a charity trance night at one of the local churches. Before I went, I sent my wolf along ahead of me, visualising him in the place I was going to be working. Afterwards, a lady called Beryl came up to me and said, 'You know, before you came into the room I saw a great big Alsatian.' Well, wolves aren't that common in the UK so I could understand her mistaking the wolf for an Alsatian.

Negativity and pain are out there constantly. We are surrounded by fear and jealousy. Before I did this exercise I would feel quite overwhelmed in crowds. I would feel ill and faint. Until I had my wolf, I didn't like going into a city. I know that many people will have had similar feelings.

When your confidence is low, other people can sense it. Predators prey on fear, so if you start sending out strong energy from yourself that shows you're not afraid, they are less likely to trouble you. I would often find the protective animal for a person to use to build up this inner strength. You can use it in all sorts of situations, for instance, when walking somewhere alone at night.

Norma, the friend I mentioned earlier, went on holiday to New York with her daughter. She always used to like travelling on local transport rather than in taxis. They'd been out late one evening and missed the last train home. At the station a big, heavy guy came up to her and demanded her purse. She's well into her sixties but she looked straight up at him and said, 'Purse? What purse? I haven't got one,' and he said, 'Oh, ok,' and just walked away.

On a lighter note, here in Spain I use my protective animal because the local sellers of tablecloths are very persistent. I put my wolf beside me at the table and they usually just walk by and don't even bother!

People who work with their dreams will have a greater under-standing of using mental images than those who will only accept the solid world that we live in. To anyone who has an open mind, this way of working can bring such joy and freedom it's well worth pursuing.

CHAPTER TWELVE

Final Words

Introduction

Death is indeed not the end of everything.

Knowing that there is an afterlife actually makes it easier to cope with the death that touches us all within life – the death of those we love, of parts of ourselves, of times and relationships and things we have treasured.

Life is a series of deaths. And we survive them. If we are wise, we are constantly moving onwards. We cannot stay the same. We are constantly learning about ourselves and others, and the world around us. We change and grow. We emerge from life's experiences a little different, a little wiser, a little closer to the recognition of our own true being. We move from place to place, our appearance changes, we take on different roles and identities, we lose relationships and find new ones and, with them, new aspects of ourselves.

When we lose one thing, we gain another. In fact, every end is just another beginning. Leaving our pain, we find our joy. Losing our body, we gain our spirit.

For this reason, an awareness of life after death – the knowledge that we continue to exist after the death of our physical body – must change not only our attitude to death, but also to life itself.

When we leave this world we carry with us, in our spirit, our energy and our mind, all that we have ever been. We hold on to all that we have achieved – our joys, our successes, our wonderful and loving memories of this time on earth. All will still exist within us.

In just the same way, if we have not yet been able to release it, if we hold on to the pain and fears and sorrows that we have experienced in this life, then these too will still exist within us. We will carry over that pain into the other world.

We can only set ourselves free from the conflict, pain and self-doubt of this life on earth if we are willing to honestly look at ourselves. We all need to do our inner work. That means admitting things about ourselves which we would rather not acknowledge, overcoming fears which we would rather not face, in order to release the love and joy and spontaneity that is part of the human psyche, part of our innate being.

We all have a spirit, even now while we are here on earth. Becoming aware of our spirituality allows us to become what we individually and uniquely are, to find within ourselves the capacity to love, to feel compassion for ourselves and others, and to discover our true purpose in life.

If we do this, then the transition that we call death, the moment at which we pass from this world into the next, will hold no fear. It will bring not shock and sorrow, but joy and excitement, a sense of coming home. It will be not an end, but another beginning – another step on our journey towards the source of all life and of all love.

Slaying the Dragon

In my workshops, I often used to quote the poet Guillaume Apollinaire's beautiful words:

> 'Come to the edge.'
> 'We can't. We're afraid.'
> 'Come to the edge.'
> 'We can't. We will fall!'
> 'Come to the edge.'
> And they came.
> And he pushed them.
> And they flew.

At some time or other, we all need someone to push us. Out of our comfort zone, or our habits, or our self-limiting beliefs. We all need someone to encourage us to find our next step.

The hardest part of life is overcoming our own dark shadows. Yet when we look more closely at them most are simply different mani-festations of fear – fear of the unknown, fear of ridicule or failure, even fear of success. Once we can do battle with that fear, then we are capable of anything.

For many of us fear has existed throughout our lives. From child-hood we learned to be fearful rather than to trust and believe in ourselves. Growing up, I always remember being chided, 'Don't do that. What will the neighbours think?'

In August 2002, I was in hospital following a major operation, and there were three of us on the ward. Our scars were very painful but we had a hilarious time.

Dave and I had previously been talking with a friend, Helen, about what regrets all of us had, and mine were that I'd never taken up art or learned to play an instrument. Helen asked, 'What instrument?' and I said, 'The clarinet.' It just came out, I'd never consciously thought of it before. Helen said, 'Well, why don't you get one?'

Shortly afterwards, Dave gave me a clarinet for my birthday and I started going to music lessons and art classes.

So, in the hospital, I was telling them this. One of the women had four children and finances were obviously a problem, but she said that she'd always yearned to play the violin. When I asked her why she didn't try, she said, 'It seems so silly.' I suggested that maybe her family could club together to buy her a violin for Christmas. When I left hospital there were tears in her eyes. She said, 'You've no idea how much our chat has helped.' I do hope that she did start to play – and to live her life the way she truly wanted to.

The vast majority of people that I've come across, both personally and in workshops, have been afraid to live their dreams – partly because they don't have the confidence, partly because society has taught us that we have to be the best at everything. At school we're not taught to enjoy learning for ourselves, but merely to pass exams. If you don't get qualifications you're seen as a failure. For many people that sense of failure stays with them throughout their lives, and this discourages them from trying what they've always longed to do.

But we don't have to be brilliant at it; we just need to do it – whatever makes us feel alive. I'll never be another Acker Bilk and my art will never get to the Tate, but playing and painting give me enormous pleasure.

We need to be individuals, to do our own thing, and not worry about what other people think of us. We are not stereotypes, we all have our own unique abilities and talents and interests. If we follow our intuition and find our own inner passions, we will have a wonderful gift for the rest of our lives.

In my workshops, I'd often say, 'We're all going to make mistakes today, and maybe make fools of ourselves. I'll make a lot of mistakes and make a complete fool of myself – and I don't care a jot! But if you want to leave, put your hand up now. That's fine.'

Some people find it hard to allow themselves not to get it right first time. But they need to ask themselves, is it really that bad if they make a mistake? Will they still be worrying about it at the end of the week or in a month's time or at the end of the year?

Freedom of mind is the greatest gift that we can have. And the greatest gift that we can give to our children is the freedom to be themselves. We can guide them and hopefully instil in them some spiritual and moral values. But the most important thing for each person is to be genuine, honest, and true to himself. If we accept what we are, then we can stop trying so hard to be what we think other people want us to be.

When my son Stuart was little, he used to ask me to wear a pinnie and a skirt like other mums. When we moved into our last house he was ten. I thought, 'Ok, I'll give it a go.' So I put a pinnie on – I couldn't go so far as wearing a skirt – and I went round polishing and cleaning and doing the housework. I got the children's sports kit washed and ironed on time and made scones for when they came home from school. I tried to be the mum I thought he wanted.

After three weeks, he and his sister, Kerrie, came up to me and said, 'Mum, can we have our mum back?' They were fed up, they couldn't cope with the new orderly me. Thank God, because it was driving me crazy!

In mediumship too, I wouldn't take on an idea unless it felt right and made sense to me. There are so many rituals and myths that, when you first start, you imagine that that's the way it's got to be.

Later, you think, 'Hang on, this doesn't make sense,' and you start to question things. Now, I take the view that what I believe makes sense for me. If other people think something else, that's fine. That's their truth. We all have to find our own truth.

Sometimes we have to break out of the confines and constraints of conventional beliefs. Most original thoughts and great advances have been made by those who stepped beyond the accepted ideas of their time. They were derided, they made mistakes along the way and yet, as a result of their thinking, things changed. Otherwise we'd all still believe that the earth is flat!

What's important is that you grow in your mind, and use your intelligence – we've all got it. Trusting yourself, accepting that you're going to make mistakes, you will find that inner voice of wisdom. This will help you to truly know yourself, and will guide you towards your innermost needs and desires.

Henry Van Dyke, the American theologist, wrote: 'Some people are so afraid to die that they never begin to live.' I certainly don't want to have regrets when I get to the other side.

There is life after death, but there is also life in life. When we pass to the spirit world we shed an overcoat. But we also need to shed an overcoat here, whilst we're on this earth.

We owe it to our own spirit to grow as much as we possibly can. That means accepting our own needs, our weaknesses and frailties, and the fact that we all make mistakes – simply because we're human.

To me, spirituality does not mean being kind and considerate just to others, but to yourself as well. Sometimes we care so much for others that we neglect ourselves. We devote our lives to our family or friends or the people we work with, and we forget that we too are spirit, that we have a life, and that life is an adventure.

How many times have we looked forward to a night in for ourselves – a long hot bath, reading a book, or an evening in the garden, only to get a phone call from someone to go and baby-sit, or a friend who needs to talk? Not wanting to appear selfish, we forego our own needs.

We don't take time for our hobbies and interests, or enough quiet time simply to be alone.

Much of the envy we feel when we see someone successfully following their dreams arises because we're not doing what we want to be doing, we're not following our own dreams. Much of the negativity that we feel towards others is a result of our sense of inadequacy and frustration at not realising our own potential.

Life isn't made up of big events. It's a series of small incidents, of simple moments. We can all change our lives and make them more joyful by taking small steps, facing small fears, grasping new possibilities. By pursuing little dreams without fear of failure we allow our spirit to grow.

It's never too late to start something new. People have said to me, for instance, 'Oh, I'd love to learn to dance, but I'm too old for all that now.' We're as old as we think we are. If you're seventy and you feel like learning to dance, then why not go ahead and give it a try?

My godmother, Lily Taylor, is a wonderful woman. It wasn't until she was sixty that she learned to drive. Then to swim. And then she took up art. Sometimes I'd pop down to see her. I'd go in the house when she'd just come back from the shops, her coat still on and already busy painting. In fact she produced some wonderful pictures. She's in her late eighties now but she's still willing to have a go at anything. She gets so much fun from life and is so enthusiastic. She is truly young at heart.

We can have as much fun in the spirit world as we can have here. We will be able to dance and swim and travel wherever we like. We will be able to do whatever we want to do – as long as we believe that we can. We need only to accept that, through the power of the mind, all is possible. Our mind creates our reality in the afterlife just as it does while we live in this material and physical world.

When people in the spirit world communicate to us, they are using the power of the mind. They send out their thoughts and energy to us and, through the power of our own mind, we can sense them.

In charity demonstrations we often used to play the song, 'I Just Called To Say I Love You.' Often, when the spirit world want to talk to us, that's all they want to say – 'I'm still here, and I love you.' Most of us don't say those things often enough in life. How many times do we think of phoning someone, only we get tied up in work or chores? And then the next week or month we find the person is ill and we've never got round to making that phone call?

Communication is one of the most important things in life. Whether it's phoning someone to say, 'I've been thinking about you, I miss you,' or, when someone upsets you, to tell him, 'Hey look, I've got a problem with this.'

Too often we use words we don't mean; we get into the habit of not expressing our true feelings.

Yet telling people that we love them and appreciate them brings joy to all of us. Admitting our mistakes avoids unnecessary guilt and resentment and conflict. We set ourselves free and spread a little of our light into the world, by being true to ourselves and honest to others. It's wonderful to be able to say sorry from the heart, and thank you when you mean it, with energy and with love.

By becoming aware of our inner fears and feelings, by making small changes within ourselves, we can make our own world a better place. By realising, while we're here on earth, that the world of spirit also exists, we come closer to understanding and appreciating the many different aspects of ourselves.

We all have a guiding light within us – the inner wisdom that knows who we really are, and all that we can truly be.

There are those in the spirit world who are always ready to help us on our spiritual journey, to help us to make that bridge between the two worlds.

We only have to look, listen, and open our hearts and minds – and we will find it.

Conclusion

I suppose there is one thing for certain: we are all going to die.

Our physical body *will* perish, but our souls, our minds, our personalities, will live on.

When we go on the greatest journey of our lives, those that we have loved and lost will be there to greet us.

People ask, 'Will I go to Heaven?' The answer is that so much depends on the state of your own mind. Bitterness, anger and jealousy will not disappear in death. We can best ensure that we will arrive in Heaven by looking deeply at ourselves now, by taking responsibility for our own words and actions. Acknowledging our jealousy and bitterness, we can diminish their power over us.

If we can put pride to one side and say sorry for words said and deeds done, then, when the time comes for us to take that journey, we can all be at peace.

Remember that while we're here, we already have help at hand. We all have the spirit within. There is always someone out there in the spirit world to guide us.

If we make quiet time in our busy lives to listen to the spirit within, and if, through the power of prayer, we reach out to those in the spirit world, then our lives will become fuller, richer, and more rewarding.

And we will truly dance in the joy of spirit.

Acknowledgements

MacMillan Publishers Limited, for permission to reprint from Douglas Adams, *So Long, And Thanks For All The Fish,* first published by Pan Books Ltd, London, 1984.

Toni and Marty Jourard, for permission to reprint from Sidney Jourard: 'Be careful in your choice of hypnotists.'

Acknowledgements and thanks from Teresa to:
Graham Crook, for editing and encouraging; for his love and faith and constant support;
Greg Dark, my mentor, for his talent, insight and impeccable advice;
Jean Kendall, for her faith and endless generosity;
Anna Sirl, my sister and ally, for a life-time of treasures;
Jeff Sirl, for his encouragement, and for believing in possibility;
Richard Noon, for his humour and big-hearted scepticism;
Marcus Vinnicombe, for laughter and magic and for keeping me sane;
Richard Marshall, for mystery and beautiful music;
Annie Jury, Amy Young, Neil Kelly, Maggie Wilkinson, Al Noon, Bree Vickers Krabbe, Frances Pearce, Janet Garrett and Avril Watson for sharing ideas and tears, laughter and dreams;
Madeleine Webber, Heidi Mussigbrodt and Anne Breuer, for their long-distance love and encouragement over many years;
David Kinchin, George Andrew and John Cannon, of the Writers' Bureau, for their knowledge, guidance and positivity.

Acknowledgements and thanks from Sue to:
My children, Kerrie and Stuart, for allowing me to be me. I love you both.
Mark Jewell-Harrison, my son-in-law, for his kindness and generosity;
Ann Anderton, the finest astrologer I know, for her constant support and encouragement;

Doreen Boyle, for always being there for me;

Jean Kendall, for her help and friendship;

Nora Shaw, a big curtsey to you;

Debbie Eastnick and Jenny Stove, for your across-the-miles friendship and loyalty;

Graham Lymer, for the wonderful communication from my dad. It made such a difference;

My students, who have given me such joy. Helping you has helped me so much;

And last but not least, *San Lo*. What would I do without you?

Our greatest thanks to:

Lawrence McDermott, our wonderful publisher, for making this book possible;

Roger Marshall, our agent, for his encouragement and organisation;

Linda Perkins, for her energy and enthusiasm;

Julian Day, for his excellent editorial advice;

Grant Shipcott, for design and typesetting;

Michael Shaw, author photos.

Contact Us

Questions and comments: we can be contacted at
www.danceinthejoyofspirit.com